SPIRALING
UP

SPIRALING
UP

Discover Financial Serenity,
Make Work Optional, and
Live Happily in Retirement

STEVEN MEDLAND

HOUNDSTOOTH
PRESS

SPIRALING UP

Discover Financial Serenity, Make Work Optional, and Live Happily in Retirement

ISBN   978-1-5445-2860-1 *Hardcover*
           978-1-5445-2861-8 *Paperback*
           978-1-5445-2862-5 *Ebook*

For Audrey and Conrad—

my wonderful daughter and son,

and my inspiration.

Contents

Introduction

The Path to Wealth Is Simple, but Not Easy

When I was a junior in high school, the stock market crashed on October 19, 1987, a day that would go down in history as Black Monday. The Dow Jones Industrial Average lost over 22% of its value in a single day, and financial markets lost an estimated $1.7 trillion worldwide.

The next day, my high school economics teacher told my class that we should save a copy of that day's *Los Angeles Times* because we were witnessing history.

My teacher also told my class that if we saved just $4,000 every year for 40 years and invested it wisely, we could all become millionaires by age 58. I went home and asked my dad if that was true, and he said it was. Then I asked him, "Why

1

doesn't everyone do that?" He replied, "It's not easy, but with the right plan, the discipline to follow it, and enough time, just about anyone can become wealthy."

It is now decades later, and after working with hundreds of wealthy families, most who are self-made, I believe my dad's formula has withstood the test of time.

Overcoming the Powerful Forces Aligned Against Us

However, as my dad said, it's not easy. Simple, yes; easy, no. Some may have the right plan, the discipline to follow it, and enough time, but each of those elements is littered with roadblocks.

The deck is stacked against us when it comes to achieving financial and investment success. An insidious system is sabotaging our financial success, even if—and maybe especially if—we aren't aware of it.

One of those forces is *consumer culture*, or feeling compelled to spend our money on certain material goods to attain the "right," socially acceptable lifestyle. Consumption may help us temporarily feel better, but those feelings are fleeting. This is closely related to the concept of "Keeping up with the Joneses," which originated in a comic strip of the same name back in 1913, demonstrating that using your neighbors as a benchmark to acquire more and more material goods is not a new phenomenon.

The media and social media are also significant factors. The media is supported by advertisers with one goal only—to part you from your hard-earned money—and social media bombards you with an idealized view of everyone else's lifestyle. People tend to post pictures of themselves basking on a Hawaiian beach at sunset, not grinding away at the office or reaching their financial goals. These factors make us want to spend money on shiny stuff for instant gratification instead of focusing on longer-term objectives.

If these things aren't challenging enough, we also live in an era when *major structural changes are occurring in our retirement system itself.* Employers have largely stopped offering pensions, so the burden of retirement savings falls squarely on us. And this is happening in a time when the Social Security system is underfunded and systematically falling behind relative to inflation.

Another challenge most of us struggle with is our own *self-limiting beliefs.* A limiting belief is an idea we think is true, but that constrains us in some way. These are often either handed down from our parents or have developed in our minds without ever being challenged. For example, believing that you have no control over becoming wealthy would likely prevent you from trying to build wealth in the first place.

I'm Financially Successful:
Why Don't I Feel That Way?

If you have had financial success but still aren't where you want to be, you may have struggled internally with the above issues, even if you haven't been able to articulate them. If that's the case, I can assure you that you are not the only one who may be "wealthy" yet still feel anxious about your finances. And you're also not alone if you haven't understood how the above forces have been holding you back, or why you feel stuck while others around you appear to be racing ahead.

The good news is that you can overcome these challenges with the right knowledge, mindset, and skillset. Working with hundreds of families who have built their wealth gradually has taught me the rules for reaching financial security, but over time, I realized something was still missing.

I struggled with seeing objectively wealthy clients who still felt poor, and I've experienced some of the same feelings myself. However, I couldn't find any resources that addressed this disconnect directly. Wasn't there anything that explained how to build wealth and concurrently reach higher levels of contentment?

I studied the issue by talking with clients and reading literally hundreds of books, from the classics to contemporary bestsellers, with topics ranging from finance and psychology to personal growth. I wrote this book because it's the one I wish I'd had earlier on my own journey, and in the hope that it can be a valuable guide for anyone who has grappled with these same issues.

Financial Security Is Achievable, but It's Only the Beginning

Along the way, I discovered that financial security is only the starting point, and there are three higher levels of financial success. These include financial independence, financial freedom, and ultimately, financial serenity. I will discuss this in greater detail in Chapter 3, but financial serenity is essentially living in a state of financial abundance, gratitude, and tranquility.

Throughout decades as an investor and financial planner, I have only worked with a small number of individuals who live in financial serenity, a concept few have even heard of. That's probably why it's so rare. While it is possible to achieve and having wealth may help, wealth alone won't get you there.

Over time, I observed a number of principles that, when followed, lead to financial serenity. Bookstore shelves are bulging with volumes that explain how to achieve wealth in dollar terms, but few, if any, explore the principles that lead to financial serenity.

Principles and Values

Billionaire investor Ray Dalio founded Bridgewater Associates and built it into the world's largest hedge fund.

As he explains in his book, *Principles*:

> Your values are what you consider important, literally what you "value." Principles are what allow you to live a life consistent with those values. Principles connect your values to your actions; they are beacons that guide your actions, and help you successfully deal with the laws of reality. It is to your principles that you turn when you face hard choices.

In short, principles are rules or codes of conduct that can help guide our actions in times of uncertainty. The seven principles of financial serenity that I have developed are:

✓ Principle One: Focus On What You Can Control

✓ Principle Two: Accept That Wealth Is a State of Mind

✓ Principle Three: Cultivate a Growth Mindset

✓ Principle Four: Understand Your Personal Financial Statement

✓ Principle Five: Use Debt Wisely, and Pay It Off

✓ Principle Six: Develop Good Financial Habits

✓ Principle Seven: Manage Risk

The first three principles deal with our inner worlds or mindsets, and the last four deal with financial practices and strategies. Some of these principles have been around for millennia, and others are relatively new. In any case, I've seen firsthand that following each one in combination with the others is what leads to more desirable financial outcomes.

Spiraling Up to Financial Serenity

I have also seen that using these principles has a compounding effect. When we make good financial decisions, big or small, it leads to improved circumstances. Those improved circumstances lead to better opportunities, and those better opportunities open the door to even more beneficial financial decisions. This results in the virtuous cycle I call spiraling up.

This book is for those who value financial serenity and are willing to cultivate the above process to achieve it.

The first three chapters discuss the challenges we all face, followed by chapters on each of the seven principles illustrated by true client stories. I changed the names and details in each client story to protect the privacy of those involved. In most cases, I changed dollar amounts, used round numbers, and ignored taxes to make the examples easier to follow.

The final chapter is a remarkable, multigenerational true story of a family spiraling up by using each one of the principles. My ardent hope is that you also use them to achieve financial security, move to and beyond financial independence and freedom, and spiral up into financial serenity yourself.

Back to the 1987 Crash

So, what does the 1987 stock market crash have to do with spiraling up? The *Los Angeles Times* copy I mentioned above is displayed on my home office bookshelf today, serving as a reminder of my own long financial journey.

The blaring headline reads, "Stocks Plunge 508 Amid Panic: Record One-Day Decline Eclipses 1929 Market Drop." This is an excellent example of why we should be cautious about the advice we get from the media. Hearing that the crash was even worse than the 1929 drop undoubtedly scared people out of the markets.

However, after the Dow Jones Industrial Average dropped 508 points and closed at 1,739 on October 19, 1987, it recovered and ended up closing above 35,000 for the first time 34 years later in 2021. While it was not possible to invest directly in the Dow Jones Industrial Average over that entire period because there was no index fund, Ned Davis Research estimates that during those 34 years, a $100,000 initial investment in the Dow would have grown to *more than $4 million*.

Someone who had the right plan, the discipline to follow it, and enough time could have done very well during this long period of economic growth and innovation, despite the many turbulent events along the way.

Anyone who invested right after the 1987 crash and didn't look at their account again for 34 years until 2021 would be ecstatic with their account balance. However, that belies all of the challenges and ups and downs they would have faced during the interim period. That leads us to why financial success is so elusive, which is the subject of Chapter 1.

Part I

THE CHALLENGE: FINANCIAL AND INVESTING SUCCESS

Chapter 1

Why Financial Success
Is So Elusive

In October 2005, Lara and Roger Griffith bought a lottery ticket and won the equivalent of $3.6 million in today's dollars. Roger worked as an information technology manager, and Lara was a performing arts teacher at a local college. While both were well-educated, neither of them had any idea how to manage such a large sum of money.

In an interview published in the *Daily Mail* years later, Lara said, "We were so desperate not to mess it up, and it's very difficult when you have advisers coming to you in their shiny suits and flashy cars saying, 'I'll look after you, trust me.' Who do you trust?"

She then added, "We were told not to put all our eggs in one basket, so we decided to invest in property and business. We thought we were doing everything right." They invested in two rental properties, the stock market, and a beauty salon.

However, after Roger quit his job, they bought their dream home for about $1.6 million, along with a brand-new convertible Porsche and Lexus SUV. They enrolled their two daughters in private school at a combined cost of $40,000 per year. They also started going on shopping sprees for jewelry and designer clothes, and they embarked on lavish first-class vacations to Dubai, Monaco, and Rome.

Five years later, in 2010, as the economy was just starting to recover from the global financial crisis, their beauty salon was still hemorrhaging money. Then, their dream home was devastated by a fire. Because they were underinsured, they had to pay for temporary accommodations for the seven months it took to repair it.

Their poor investment decisions, overspending, and failure to manage risk resulted in them losing every penny of the $3.6 million within six years.

In many of the "riches to rags" lottery stories we hear, we often assume that the people who lose their lottery winnings are unsophisticated or uneducated. However, this story illustrates how anyone is vulnerable to those losses.

Lara and Roger were intelligent, educated, and were (at least initially) sincerely committed to making the money last. They should have been set for life. How could a couple with all of those advantages fail so spectacularly after receiving such a windfall?

This leads us to the larger question: if we all say we want financial success, why do so few of us ever actually achieve it?

Unfortunately, this disconnect exists for numerous reasons, including consumer culture, the media, and social media. It's also challenging to overcome instant gratification and lifestyle creep in an era when pensions are going away and we are increasingly responsible for our own retirement savings. These factors, especially when combined with our own financial self-limiting beliefs, can sabotage our financial success.

Programmed to Consume

The fact is, we are practically programmed from birth to consume at, if not beyond, our means. All media, including newspapers, radio, magazines, and television, have business models built on advertising. This business model only works if they can draw more viewers, digital marketing impressions, and viewing hours, and if those viewers then buy the advertised products. Buying more and more is good for the media, their advertisers, and the brands themselves—but it's not good for your net worth or financial well-being.

This is all powerfully reinforced by television and film consistently correlating your self-esteem with how much stuff you accumulate and the prestige of fancy homes, racy cars, exotic travel, and other luxury goods.

Consumerism is also emphasized through endless testimonials and endorsements by celebrities we admire, as is routinely seen in advertising and social media.

In the newest iteration, social media influencers drive their followers to consume. The primary qualification of these influencers is often simply their follower counts. Most have no actual expertise in the areas they promote. Yet they flaunt—and the advertising industry promotes—designer clothes, indulgent spas, extravagant vacations, luxury cars, pricey cosmetic surgery, and flashy jewelry and accessories. Then, legions of followers go out and buy them like preprogrammed robots.

Regrettably, I've been guilty of this myself. Have you ever paid full retail price for a small $500 handbag for your significant other or yourself? Ugh—not an experience I plan to repeat.

The Griffiths also fell into this trap, only to learn that unconscious spending leads to an empty feeling and stress. When asked about her penchant for Louis Vuitton handbags, Lara Griffith said, "Actually, it didn't feel so fabulous to be able to pay for whatever we wanted. We felt scared. You are constantly thinking, 'Is this wrong? Will we lose it? Is this the right decision to make? How long will it last?' We were always stressed."

This dynamic of conspicuous consumption, now deeply embedded in the American psyche, is exemplified by the selfie culture. Armies of consumers are devouring these items, but many don't have the discipline to delay gratification for them, choosing instead to rack up credit card debt and postpone saving.

The real tragedy here is that few of these luxury goods make their owners happy for more than a day, and even then, they're not as happy as they would be having a larger cash cushion in the bank and a well-funded plan for a comfortable retirement. In fact, the empty feeling that typically follows extravagant purchases only fuels the next one. But the siren song of rampant consumerism is extremely potent.

How many TV and movie characters or influencers do you ever see focusing on saving and investing for retirement? Probably none, because retirement is 20 to 40 years away for most of these characters and deemed boring.

Most people wish they could save more, have a well-funded retirement plan, and have less junk overflowing in their closets and garages. It's just not easy to get there when they're being bombarded by highly sophisticated consumption and marketing messages around the clock.

For most, 90% of the challenge to live within one's means, not overspend, and follow a disciplined savings and investment regimen is not an *inability* to do things like setting up automatic monthly transfers into their savings and investments. It is an *unwillingness* to give up the feelings, the dopamine hit, and the ego boost from consuming grown-up toys, overspending on luxuries, and planning over-the-top vacations to impress friends on social media.

But once one sees the bigger picture, instead of the transitory illusion of happiness that comes from buying more stuff, it becomes nearly effortless to align financial values and behaviors.

Instant Gratification and
Financial Literacy

The ethos of the Greatest Generation, which sacrificed at home and overseas to win World War II, is steadily fading. Younger generations have increasingly learned to pursue instant gratification over the delayed rewards of pursuing loftier goals.

Schools don't teach instant gratification, but young adults learn it by example, through the media, and at home. It may be difficult for them, therefore, to delay gratification for long-term goals, such as saving for retirement, when their role models overspend and live on the financial edge.

A general lack of financial literacy is also a challenge, making it hard for many to understand how today's minor sacrifices can lead to much better future outcomes. For example, the small investments made consistently when a person is young lead to a vastly larger nest egg in retirement. Schools don't teach even the most basic personal finance concepts, and we get mixed messages from friends, the media, and parents, very few of whom seem to have it figured out.

Social Comparison and
Lifestyle Creep

Achieving financial success is even more complicated if you define success in terms of others' expectations. This is a recipe for frustration because you might be comparing yourself to someone who inherited money or had some type of a head start that you didn't.

It may sometimes be better to be lucky than good, but as we saw with Lara and Roger Griffith, even multimillion-dollar lottery winners can end up flat broke in only a matter of years. Believe it or not, roughly 70% of people who win a lottery or get a big windfall end up bankrupt in a few years, based on research from the National Endowment for Financial Education. Many of these bankruptcies are undoubtedly due to spending in a way they think wealthy people *should* spend.

We'll explore the benefit of having a wealth mindset and prosperity consciousness in the principles section later. For now, just remember that the only measure of success that matters is what's important to you and whether you're moving toward goals that are in alignment with your values on a schedule that suits you.

Even those who are financially secure have to be vigilant for other reasons. Lifestyle creep makes financial success a moving target. This phenomenon often happens when you receive a pay raise—you have extra money, which leads to increased spending to buy the next luxury good or service on your list. The Griffiths initially celebrated their lottery win sensibly with takeout Indian food and a bottle of champagne, but after they received the money, their purchases rocketed out of control.

For many Americans, spending more because of lifestyle creep means they find themselves living paycheck to paycheck again, which means they work even harder to get the next raise. The cycle continues to the point that even though they're eventually working extremely long hours and earning significantly more than before, they never get off the treadmill of living paycheck to paycheck.

Contrast this with someone who earns a pay raise, does not increase consumption, and simply banks or invests the additional aftertax income. Who's likely happier in the long run?

Employer Retirement Plans and Social Security

The framework underlying our retirement system itself is also changing. Do you know anyone who retired from a company after 30 or 40 years with a pension and a gold watch? If so, they're likely in their 80s now because pensions have largely gone away, at least for nongovernment employees.

Research from the Social Security Administration confirms that, for the last three decades, there has been a steady decline in the percentage of workers covered by traditional defined benefit (DB) pension plans that pay lifetime income. This lifetime income is also known as a lifetime annuity, and these DB plans are often based on years of employment and final salary. The result can be a valuable income stream that increases with inflation, but this idyllic retirement scenario is becoming increasingly rare.

There is little job security, and the pensions promised to public workers—including teachers, law enforcement, and firefighters—are just that: promises by politicians. The simple math of those pensions shows they are not sustainable. The nation's largest public pension plan, California Public Employees Retirement System (CalPERS), announced it would decrease its assumed rate of return to 7%. Still, even that appears to be an unrealistically high rate of return in an era when 30-year government bonds are only paying around 2% per year and stock market returns are volatile.

If you don't have a pension, you may have a 401(k) plan, but that comes with its own set of challenges. How do you know in which funds to invest your contributions if you're not an investment professional? Human resources departments are generally forbidden to give investment guidance, so where do you turn for unbiased advice?

Those who are relying on Social Security to rescue their retirement are in for disappointment. The benefits are surreptitiously reduced every year with complex inflation adjustments deliberately designed to minimize the real value of the amount sent to recipients. And just like other state pension schemes, the math shows Social Security is not sustainable without significant tax increases or a reduction in benefits.

Even for those who study financial success strategies, the rules are constantly changing, and the nature of financial knowledge is use-it-or-lose-it. It can be overwhelming to keep up with tax law changes, the latest estate planning techniques, and new investment tactics. Despite these challenges, investing itself is presented, mainly through advertisements, as something a child can do merely with the click of a button.

How We Get In Our Own Way

Self-limiting beliefs are some of the most significant obstacles to achieving financial success. Lara and Roger Griffith apparently shared the limiting belief that spending money would lead to happiness, but that led instead to the predictable result of near bankruptcy.

Other common limiting beliefs are: money is the root of all evil, you need to have money to make money, and you have to hurt others to become wealthy. Any of these beliefs can prevent us from reaching the level of financial success we desire. I'll go into more detail and discuss how to overcome limiting beliefs when exploring Principle Two: Accept That Wealth Is a State of Mind.

Overcoming These Challenges

In this chapter, you've seen several insidious and subtle hurdles that stand between you and your financial success. Fortunately, you'll see in later chapters that although the deck is stacked against you in many ways, you can overcome all of these challenges with awareness, knowledge, and the right skillset. That's when following the seven principles of financial serenity will come in.

Summary of Key Points

- Although most people say they want financial success, few actually achieve it.
- The disconnect between wanting and achieving financial success results from the following factors:
  - Consumer culture
  - The media and social media
  - Desire for instant gratification
  - Lifestyle creep
  - Major structural changes in our retirement system
  - Our own financial self-limiting beliefs
- While the above challenges seem daunting, we can overcome them with awareness and knowledge, and by following the principles in this book.

Learning from
Lara and Roger Griffith

We can learn from the Griffiths' cautionary tale and thrive in the face of these obstacles. For now, you have an understanding of why financial success is so hard to achieve, even though that's what everyone says they want. One of the many reasons that the Griffiths struggled was the complexity of successful investing, and that is the subject of our next chapter.

Chapter 2

Why Investing Success Seems So Difficult (But Doesn't Have to Be)

Justin Timberlake is well known as an incredibly successful entertainer, but he is not as well known for his demonstrated investment acumen. Unlike most other former Mouseketeers or boy band heartthrobs who eventually became afterthoughts, he was not only able to transition from pop star to critically acclaimed performing artist, but he also built a vast business empire.

He has made profitable investments in fashion, restaurants, a golf course, beverages, and the NBA's Memphis Grizzlies, and has an estimated net worth of over $250 million, according to the website Celebrity Net Worth.

However, even astute investors eventually learn how difficult investing can be. In 2011, Timberlake and Specific Media Group jointly purchased a stake in Myspace, a social networking site known as a precursor to Facebook, for $35 million. Despite attempts to reinvigorate the dwindling user base, Myspace continued its decline after the investment and was eventually completely overshadowed by Facebook.

If an experienced investor with a team of expert advisors can fall into a trap like this, what chance do the rest of us have?

The Challenges of Successful Investing

The truth is that investing successfully is more difficult than we are led to believe (although we'll learn in the principles section that it can be done with the right plan). We see commercials showing all types of people with zero financial or investment training clicking on phone apps and effortlessly making money buying and selling stocks.

What we don't see is the other side of these stock transactions: sophisticated Wall Street traders with access to tens of millions of dollars in technological infrastructure and expert research, all designed to capitalize on these inexperienced investors' mistakes.

Average investors are fighting an uphill battle on multiple fronts. They're up against dwindling human advice, increasingly complex markets, faster and more complex electronic trading, historically low interest rates, their own psychological blind spots, and the media.

Shrinking Commissions and Vanishing Investment Advice

Before the internet led to the democratization of stock investing, placing a trade required the services of a licensed stockbroker. Buying 100 shares of common stock would cost a commission of up to 2% of the trade. Selling those shares at a profit or loss doubled that commission.

That meant the stock value would have to increase by 4% before you would begin to make any profit, then capital gains taxes would reduce that profit. This caused any rational investor to consider stock purchases carefully, and that purchase would be reviewed and normally discussed over the phone with a licensed stockbroker.

These costs have dropped over the past several decades, but with a hidden price. Investing apps led the way, and now, most online brokerages have dropped those commission rates to zero. Accordingly, there has been a corresponding drop in credible human advice about which stocks to buy or sell based on professional analysis and the investor's goals and risk tolerance.

This drop in advice has come at a difficult time because markets are more complex, globally linked, and volatile than ever. Most investors are simply not equipped to succeed in this environment.

Trading at the Speed of Light

Algorithmic trading has increased the speed and complexity of trading. These computer algorithms use preprogrammed, automated instructions that can trade tens of thousands of times per second. You are trading against supercomputers housed one floor below stock exchanges so they can shave a nanosecond off the milliseconds required to enter buy and sell orders.

Trading hot stocks is an activity that is now remarkably similar to sports betting. In 2021, software and data aggregation company Envestnet Yodlee reported the US government COVID-19 stimulus checks funded a surge in securities trading. For many, this acted as a substitute for sports betting.

All of this is occurring against a backdrop of lowering interest rates, which means less income for bond investors and bank savings accounts.

The Incredible Shrinking Interest Rate

Banks punish savers by paying them 0.01% interest on their savings. That translates to earning all of $10 for lending the bank your $100,000 savings for an entire year. Lower savings rates, combined with bond investments paying historically low rates, force you and trillions of dollars into the stock market in hopes of greater gains, but with correspondingly far higher risk.

In addition to the above challenges, we're all faced with psychological blind spots that, if not addressed, will hinder our investment performance.

Discovering Our Blind Spots

The field of behavioral economics has discovered that, contrary to classical economics predictions, human beings are not always rational regarding their money. Since the beginning of economic studies, economists have assumed people always act rationally to increase their capital, wealth, or economic utility (how satisfying a good or commodity is to the consumer).

In 2002, Daniel Kahneman, the father of behavioral economics, won a Nobel Prize after proving that humans are not rational when it comes to their finances. This relatively new field of study helps explain why people make illogical decisions with their money, like buying cologne we don't need to get a free duffel bag, when we could have purchased a higher-quality duffel bag for a lot less money.

None of us are immune to making irrational decisions at some point. In my 20s, I bought an overpriced extended warranty for a gigantic television because it included free lifetime cleanings of the cathode ray tubes. All I had to do was unhook the rat's nest of wires, load that massive TV into my car, and drive it down to Best Buy for the free cleanings. Needless to say, I never went through the hassle. Live and learn.

In his fantastic 2011 book *Thinking: Fast and Slow*, Kahneman explains that our brains have an older, primitive area that can easily override the newer, intellectual area of our brain. The primitive part of our brain is the one screaming "SELL!" when the herd panics and the market is going down, even though we intellectually know the market trends upward over time.

This field of study has uncovered dozens of other biases, including the fact that we're genetically wired to avoid loss and pursue fast, easy gains. We buy stocks that are going up because we enjoy being part of the crowd making money. However, we're more likely to make an emotional decision to buy the stock after it's gone up, and at some point, it's probably going to at least temporarily go down. We don't like the feeling when our stock goes down, so we make an emotional decision to sell. This behavioral cycle ensures we're buying high and selling low, guaranteeing investment failure.

Investing is not just a combination of economics and our *individual* psychology. Even if we manage to identify and overcome all of our personal blind spots, *group* psychology also makes investing more difficult.

The US Federal Reserve is adept at manipulating this group psychology by lowering interest rates and bailing out entire industries. Their actions drive the markets and encourage investors to bid up stock prices, regardless of companies' fundamental values. Why worry about a company's financial health if the Fed is going to bail them out anyway? This is known as a moral hazard, and the Fed is keeping it alive and well.

The Media Is Hazardous to Your Wealth

The media—backed by hundreds of billions of dollars in revenue —is well-equipped to analyze and take advantage of these individual and group psychology biases. Marketers bombard us with messages showing that investing is easy for everyone else, and if you are not instantly making money in the market, something is wrong. Or you need to try something new, such as selling a stock that is down to buy another that is up and rising. This only fuels the fire for instant gratification.

A steady diet of mainstream news is toxic for our financial well-being. Focused and financially successful investors ignore the breathless talking heads in the 24-hour news cycle. News stations sensationalize everything to increase viewership, but successful investors realize it has little to no value in driving their investment decisions.

For the networks, the increased viewership simply means higher advertising revenue. They don't exist to help viewers become financially independent. Many of those talking heads on financial news channels have an agenda, commonly known as "talking their books," to entice you to buy the stocks or sectors they already own at lower prices so they can sell at higher prices. Believe it or not, this is legal, although certain requirements exist for disclosing what one owns. Following their advice and not getting the investing results you anticipated is not a recipe for happiness.

Carl Richards, CERTIFIED FINANCIAL PLANNER™ professional and author of *The Behavior Gap*, has a simple reminder to limit our exposure to the media, something he calls a media fast.

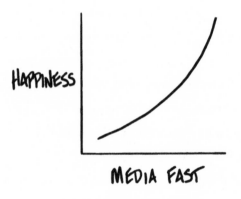

MEDIA FAST

Source: Behavior Gap, used with permission.

A media fast doesn't necessarily mean cutting out all media from our lives, and it doesn't mean burying our heads in the sand when it comes to world events and valuable news. However, it does mean being more mindful about exposing ourselves to sensationalized financial news.

The chart he created shows happiness growing exponentially by reducing media exposure, and I've found that to be true, both in my own personal experience and from clients.

He emphasizes the point in his book *The Behavior Gap: Simple Ways to Stop Doing Dumb Things with Money*. Richards writes:

> Most of the stock market coverage in the media was designed to appeal to our fantasies about getting rich quickly—our wildest financial hopes and dreams . . . Sure, investing is fun while you're making money. And it's fun to indulge in occasional daydreams about getting rich the easy way. But this is not Monopoly. This is real life. We're dealing with real money and real goals. When we forget that—when we confuse investing and entertainment—we almost always end up behaving badly. So next time you are tempted to "play the stock market" maybe you should go to the movies instead.

Beyond fantasies of fast riches, the bare, unspoken truth is that the system is carefully designed to part retail investors like you from your hard-earned dollars. With trillions at stake, you can be sure this is an actual science highly developed by some of the world's sharpest and best-paid minds. It leads to retail investors making emotional, if not genetically programmed, decisions that result in buying high and selling low.

As you will read in the chapters ahead, the good news is that while retail investors face numerous powerful forces, you can increase your wealth substantially over the years with awareness and the right savings and investment plan. Even if you waited until later in life, the principles outlined ahead are timeless in their power to ensure you build wealth.

Summary of Key Points

When it comes to investing success, nonprofessional retail investors face a number of challenges:

- The drop in commissions to zero has also come with a corresponding decrease to zero human advice from these trading platforms.
- Markets are more complex, globally linked, and changing at a faster rate than ever.
- Treating online stock investing as a substitute for sports betting has resulted in speculation and wide fluctuations in prices based on the crowd's herd mentality and emotions.
- Lower interest rates have reduced income from bank deposits and bonds to near zero, forcing investors to buy into stocks at inflated prices.
- We all have psychological blind spots that can cause us to make suboptimal investment decisions, but professional investors have advanced training and systems to help overcome such biases.
- Even if we address our own blind spots, mass crowd psychology can cause wild, irrational swings in the market that investment fundamentals alone can't explain.

- The media is primed to take advantage of our counter-productive instincts. They exploit our fears to increase their advertising revenue and the advertisers' sales—not to make us better investors.

Moving beyond These Obstacles

Justin Timberlake's story shows that investing can be a minefield for even the largest and most sophisticated investors, underscoring how ordinary investors have even more significant challenges.

Even so, with awareness, clearheaded determination, and the principles in this book, we can still overcome these disadvantages to achieve financial and investing success. But to do that, we need to know what target we're aiming for. Defining that success is the topic of our next chapter.

Chapter 3

What Is Financial Success, Anyway?

In the May 2005 edition of *The New Yorker*, Kurt Vonnegut wrote an obituary for his friend Joseph Heller. Heller was the author of *Catch-22*, a novel that sold over 10 million copies. The obituary recounts the story of the two friends talking at a party hosted by a billionaire on Shelter Island, New York.

At the party, Vonnegut asked Heller how it made him feel that their host could have made more money in one day than *Catch-22* had made in its entire history. Heller said, "I've got something he can never have."

When Vonnegut asked what that was, Heller replied, "The knowledge that I've got enough."

The concept of having enough is an underappreciated and rarely explored aspect of financial success. We all say we want financial success, but what does that really mean?

It means something different to everyone you ask, which is why it's so difficult to come up with an all-encompassing definition. Yet, without at least defining it for yourself, how can you possibly attain it?

Financial Success

Financial success is a broad term that is dependent on every individual's perspective and values.

One person's idea of financial success could be enough money to have a pleasant apartment, a reliable if modest car, a nice vacation each year, and the ability to retire at 70. This may be someone, for example, who loves his or her career teaching, which may pay below average in dollars but offers fulfillment and paid summers off.

Another's idea of financial success may be having a $10 million investment portfolio by age 60. This may be doable if that person has the skills and motivation to work 60-plus hours per week in an inevitably stressful business, earning well above average compensation, saving, and investing a significant portion consistently, starting early in their life.

The difference between the two people above comes down to their personal values. In the same way, your definition of financial success will have its roots in your values. Your values are a by-product of your life's experience, and they shape your intentions and choices for the kind of life you want to live today and in the years ahead.

Think of these values as the foundation for determining your definition of financial success. Values are subject to change and adjustment along with your varying life experiences, but they will be less likely to change significantly as the years pass. That is an element that helps differentiate values from goals, wishes, feelings, or desires.

Values, therefore, are a great starting point when defining what's important to you. Then, armed with that definition, setting your goals to reach your version of financial success becomes more straightforward. Think of financial goals as a compass to help guide you on your journey to financial success.

After discussing values, we'll discuss financial success itself, progressing from meeting basic needs to living in complete abundance, all in alignment with your values. In order to do this, we'll define the four levels of financial success, starting with financial security, then financial independence, financial freedom, and ultimately, financial serenity.

Former First Lady
Eleanor Roosevelt on Values

"To be mature you have to realize what you value most. It is extraordinary to discover that comparatively few people reach this level of maturity. They seem never to have paused to consider what has value for them. They spend great effort and sometimes make great sacrifices for values that, fundamentally, meet no real needs of their own. Perhaps they have imbibed the values of their particular profession or job, of their community or their neighbors, of their parents or family. Not to arrive at a clear understanding of one's own values is a tragic waste. You have missed the whole point of what life is for."

—*You Learn by Living: Eleven Keys for a More Fulfilling Life* by **Eleanor Roosevelt**

Values

Your values are simply characteristics or types of behavior you believe to be important in life. These are deeply held beliefs that guide how you want to live. For example, some people value achievement, and others value work–life balance, such as adequate time to raise a family. Neither one is necessarily right or wrong; what's important is that our actions align with our values.

If the person who values achievement is working 60 hours per week toward their next promotion, they're probably going to feel a sense of well-being. On the other hand, the person who values balance would only have that same sense of well-being if they were dedicating sufficient time to work and family and other activities they enjoy, such as travel, time with friends, or volunteer work.

That's why it's essential to match your actions to your values, whatever they might be. This is also where goals come in. The person who values achievement may set a goal to become a corporate vice president by age 45. As long as that person is taking actions consistent with that goal, they'll feel a sense of fulfillment. Working long hours or coming into the office on the weekend are not viewed as a sacrifice, just part of the corporate game. The opposite would be true for someone who values work–life balance. (If you are curious about exploring your values in greater detail, please see Appendix A: Values Worksheet, which will help you discover your top three personal values.)

Because you're reading this book, your values likely include things like security, independence, freedom, and serenity, which correspond to the four levels of financial success. While I didn't invent any of the following terms and various definitions exist for each, I'll outline them below in an order I think makes the most sense.

Financial Security

Financial security is living below your means and having a solid financial foundation. It means fundamentally having enough income to meet expenses consistently, and it involves having money saved to cover emergencies and future needs. It also means having an estate plan and insurance in place to protect your assets, your income, and your loved ones.

The goal at this level is to meet your current needs, save for the future, and have a plan to move forward when the unexpected happens, in addition to having a plan to achieve future financial goals.

Financial security may also mean you have passive income that covers some of your basic living expenses. Passive income comes from regular earnings that are not from your job. It could come from investment income, a rental property, or affiliate marketing from writing a blog.

Financial Independence

Financial independence is the next step above financial security. This means you're still covering all of the areas outlined above, but now you've met the goal of being able to stop working if you choose to because your passive income covers all of your expenses for your current lifestyle.

If you are financially independent, you don't need to rely on income from a job to meet your financial obligations. As financial blogger Michael Kitces says, "Being financially independent is about being independent from the *need* to work, which then opens the door to more productive conversations about whether we *want* to work, and what *meaningful* work might be."

Financial Freedom

Financial freedom is the next level beyond financial independence. This is where you meet the above criteria, but your passive income covers all of your expenses for your *ideal* lifestyle. It means freedom to buy what you want, live where you desire, and gift money to whomever you choose or whatever causes you support.

Interestingly, financial freedom doesn't just include the "freedom to" do what you want; it also includes "freedom from" the things you don't want. It provides freedom from bill collectors, from debt, and from unfulfilling work.

Does that make financial freedom the highest goal? For many people, it does.

However, it's possible to have financial freedom but still feel like there's never enough. It's possible to have financial freedom but not appreciate what you have because you're so focused on what you *want*. It's possible to have financial freedom but still worry excessively about finances, investments, and the latest news. What good is financial freedom if you're not truly free?

Financial Serenity

Just as financial freedom lies beyond financial independence, financial serenity lies beyond financial freedom. Financial serenity is living in a state of financial abundance, gratitude, and tranquility.

Financial security, financial independence, and financial freedom are all external, while financial serenity is internal. The first three levels are defined by numbers that show up in your bank account, investment statements, and financial records relative to financial obligations, bills, and desires. Financial serenity, on the other hand, is something you *feel*.

Pure and simple, it is a state of mind. However, the extreme scarcity of this mindset is not surprising when considering the relentless 24/7 bombardment of media messages received everywhere we look, listen, or click.

In essence, those messages are that we always need to get more, spend more on bigger and more expensive toys, vacation homes, and cars regardless of our financial achievements. Then, when we have those things, we need a private jet, mansion, and mega yacht to fill some perceived hole in our lives or self-image. Those who live in financial serenity develop the ability to ignore these messages and understand the difference between wants and needs.

Financial serenity is an inside game. Accordingly, the outward signs are not necessarily visible. However, things like substantial charitable giving and deliberately living far below one's means often signify living in financial serenity.

A 2018 *Architectural Digest* article reported Warren Buffett, one of the world's wealthiest men, drives a 2014 Cadillac XTS with an original starting price of $55,000. Jeff Bezos, another of the world's richest men, drives a used Honda Accord. Alice Walton, the world's richest woman at $50 billion, drives a 2006 Ford F-150 pickup, which cost around $40,000 new. You get the idea—they do not need to impress anyone or consume merely because they can.

While those are extreme examples, it's a great reminder that the rest of us don't need to overconsume to impress anyone either. Understanding that is just the beginning of cultivating a sense of complete internal contentment.

Financial serenity means focusing on abundance rather than what's missing. In fact, it's theoretically possible to live like a Zen monk, relinquish all material goods, and achieve financial serenity. With the right mindset, one could find abundance, gratitude, and tranquility with only the bare necessities to sustain life.

But, that's not what I'm advocating. I've lived through periods of both financial scarcity and abundance, and I, and virtually all the clients I have counseled over the years, believe that all things being equal, it's better to have financial abundance. As the old joke goes, "I've been rich, and I've been poor. Rich is better."

I also believe it's more realistic to achieve financial serenity if you first achieve some form of financial security, financial independence, or financial freedom. That's why we'll not only focus on mindset and our inner world but also simple yet powerful financial tools, practices, and strategies.

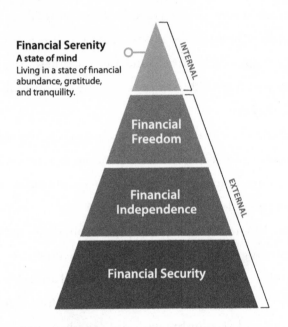

Financial Freedom
Passive income covers all expenses for your *ideal* lifestyle
Freedom to buy what you want, live where you desire, and gift money to whomever you choose or any causes you support.

Financial Independence
Passive income is meeting financial obligations
Enables you to stop working if desired or to pursue more meaningful work.

Financial Security
Living below your means
Meeting current needs and saving for your future, with a solid cash cushion for the unexpected and a plan to achieve financial goals.

The Challenge Ahead

Financial serenity is the pinnacle of the financial success hierarchy and, ultimately, where we want to be. However, reaching financial serenity is not easy, as previously discussed, largely due to the messages we get from advertisers, consumer culture, and social media.

These forces exploit the fact that we've evolved over millions of years to be dissatisfied with our current situation and always strive for more. Such discontent is one of the things that has made the human race so innovative and prosperous, but it also has a downside. That constant feeling of dissatisfaction makes it hard to recognize that we have enough, even when we're living in great abundance.

Rising to the Challenge

Joseph Heller's wisdom about having enough is a great starting point when considering financial success, but getting to financial serenity requires more thought and action.

The good news is, after decades of working as an advisor with hundreds of clients, I have identified seven principles—with corresponding practical financial planning techniques—that lead to financial success, including the holy grail, financial serenity. They are outlined in the following seven chapters, which will help you chart your course. While they are simple, they are not easy for most. However, as you begin to apply them, further implementation becomes easier as each principle builds on the ones before it.

It's important to note that achieving financial serenity and spiraling up financially should be viewed as a journey instead of a destination. An apt analogy may be the Buddhist focus on achieving enlightenment, a state of inner peace and wisdom. Some argue nobody has ever achieved permanent enlightenment; it's more of a North Star or an ideal state to pursue. However, many believe it is something regular human beings can at least temporarily experience.

Financial serenity is similar in that we are aiming for something extraordinary but not readily achievable. We may temporarily reach a state of financial serenity, but we could easily be knocked out of that state if, for example, a natural disaster causes tens of thousands of dollars of damage to our home or we unexpectedly lose our job. The key is to understand that financial serenity exists, we can experience it, and we can get back to it when knocked off of our path.

This will require a disciplined understanding of these principles. It will also require solid, though not perfect, implementation and the willingness to adapt and make changes as life inevitably throws us the occasional curveball in the form of disruptions to career, health, and family.

Summary of Key Points

- Because financial success is a broad term that is dependent on every individual's perspective and values, it's important to define it for yourself so you know what you're aiming for.
- Your values are characteristics or types of behavior that are important to you, and they serve as the foundation for your definition of financial success.
- You can use Appendix A: Values Worksheet to discover your top three personal values.
- The four general levels of financial success are:
  - Financial Security—Living below your means and meeting current needs with a plan for the future.
  - Financial Independence—Passive income is meeting your financial obligations.
  - Financial Freedom—Passive income covers all expenses for your *ideal* lifestyle.
  - Financial Serenity—Living in a state of financial abundance, gratitude, and tranquility.
- Achieving financial serenity and spiraling up financially is a journey, not a destination.

What Comes Next

I'll cover the seven principles in the following chapters and tie all of them together in Chapter 11: Lessons of a Lifetime. Then the appendices will list the resources available to help support and guide you on your journey, ranging from exploring your values and recommended reading to how to select the right financial planner, if you so choose.

Now we'll begin Part II with the first principle, which is focusing on what you can control.

Part II

THE SOLUTION: SPIRALING UP WITH THE SEVEN PRINCIPLES OF FINANCIAL SERENITY

Chapter 4

Principle One:
Focus On What You
Can Control

"You have power over your mind—not outside events.
Realize this, and you will find strength."

"If you are distressed by anything external,
the pain is not due to the thing itself, but to your estimate of it;
and this you have the power to revoke at any moment."

—**Marcus Aurelius**, Roman emperor from
161 to 180 and a Stoic philosopher

"Peace comes from within. Do not seek it without."

—**Buddhist teaching**

"Psychologists will tell you your ability to put your
mind where you want, when you want, for how long you want
(they call it a spotlight of attention) is the most important
hallmark of flourishing human beings."

—**Brian Johnson**, Founder of Optimize

"Just keep in mind: the more we value things outside
our control, the less control we have."

—**Epictetus**, first-century Greek Stoic philosopher

Lessons from a Naval Officer
and Philosopher

James Stockdale was a US Navy pilot who, on September 9, 1965, was shot down on his third combat tour in Vietnam. He was the senior-ranking naval prisoner of war in the notorious Hanoi Hilton POW camp. Stockdale was imprisoned for seven and a half years, including four years in solitary confinement. During his imprisonment, he was beaten, placed in leg irons, and tortured repeatedly.

Three years before he was shot down, Stockdale had been a graduate student at Stanford University. That's when his favorite philosophy professor gave him one of Epictetus's books, called *The Enchiridion*, as a farewell present before he left to go back to sea. Epictetus was a physically disabled Greek slave who became a prominent Stoic philosopher in Rome during the first century AD.

Epictetus taught that:

> The chief task in life is simply this: to identify and separate matters so that I can say clearly to myself which are externals not under my control, and which have to do with the choices I actually control. Where then do I look for good and evil? Not to uncontrollable externals, but within myself to the choices that are my own.

In other words, he taught his students to focus on what they can control and ignore what is outside of their control. This was the most vital practice of the ancient Stoics, and the Christian Serenity Prayer, Buddhist manuscripts, and Jewish philosophy have also expressed this wisdom.

As Stockdale drifted downward after ejecting from his plane, he heard bullets ripping his parachute canopy and watched as about a dozen men from the town prepared to gang tackle and pummel him upon landing, which resulted in them breaking his left leg. In the last few seconds before landing, he whispered to himself, "Five years down there at least. I'm leaving the world of technology and entering the world of Epictetus."

He accepted the fact that most things were about to be out of his control, including his physical environment, food, and his own body. However, he also knew that his thoughts, attitude, and judgments would remain entirely in his control.

This core tenant of Stoic philosophy is what Stockdale credited with keeping him alive for all those years in captivity. He not only survived—he also used his position as the senior-ranking officer in the prison to coordinate the resistance efforts and improve the morale and cohesion of his fellow prisoners. He did this in part by creating and enforcing a code of conduct outlining expected behavior and secret communications methods.

Stockdale went on to receive the Medal of Honor, become President of the Naval War College, and earn the rank of a three-star admiral.

While we would never expect to find ourselves in such dire conditions as Stockdale did, the principle of focusing on what we can control is valuable in many areas of our lives, including our finances.

Why Our Focus Matters

The wisdom of Epictetus and Emperor Marcus Aurelius has survived two thousand years because it is so effective, and that's why the first principle of financial serenity is focusing on what you can control. The other six principles of financial serenity build on this fundamental principle.

A life focused on areas out of our control is a life likely doomed to frustration. Conversely, a life focused on what lies within our control leads to better results, tranquility, and success.

For example, none of us can control traffic, but we can control when we leave and whether we have an excellent audiobook at the ready while we drive.

Similarly, we need to make clear what areas of our finances are within and outside our control. We have control over our saving and spending. We also control our asset allocation and investment choices, keeping investment costs low, and managing our behavior like buying low and selling high.

We have some control over our career earnings and duration, as well as our lifespans, based on the choices we make throughout our lives.

Market returns, politicians, and tax policy are entirely out of our control. However, most people spend more time worrying about those things than the areas where they do have control.

I've seen what happens to those who retire then sit in front of the television consuming a steady diet of the latest sensational news stories. Over time, this magnifies their worries and destroys their health and equanimity. Those who focus on achieving financial serenity avoid overconsuming news.

Whatever your financial, cable, or network news consumption, try measuring it, cutting it in half for a week, and seeing how you feel. Take that number of hours, and cut it in half again the following week. See if you or your family notices a difference in whether you sleep better, feel more positive, and relax more. You can even buy an inexpensive blood pressure monitor at your drugstore or online and see if your numbers drop a few points over that period.

Ignore Things Outside of Your Control

If you ignore the things outside your control, you'll have more time and energy to focus on the things within your control. To start, you'll have the bandwidth to reflect on your financial values. What is important to you? Do you want to spend more time with family, be able to travel the world, fund your children's education, or give back through your favorite charity? Defining your financial values allows you to develop goals to live in accordance with those values.

Worrying about how an armed conflict halfway around the world could potentially affect the price of gold will not get you where you want to go. Focusing instead on what you can control turns an endless number of overwhelming, complex choices into a straightforward exercise. If your goal is to pay your child's college expenses, you can take the right actions to make that a reality. Once you've defined what you want to accomplish, it becomes a relatively simple math problem.

Taking Action

If, for example, your goal is to save $100,000 before your child or grandchild starts college, it's possible to use an online financial calculator to determine how much to save monthly to get there. These calculations will, of course, have to include reasonable assumptions.

If the child is three years old, that means that there are 15 more years until he or she likely starts college. It is possible to calculate that you would need to save about $400 per month to achieve that goal, using a conservative investment return assumption of 4%. Then, it's a matter of setting up a 529 tax-advantaged college savings account and establishing a $400 per month automatic transfer into that account.

You would need to monitor the investments over the 15 years, and you could make adjustments over time, based on whether or not the account is growing as planned. If returns exceed 4% for, say, the first 10 years, you might be able to reduce the $400 monthly contributions in the five years before college.

The point is to focus on what is in your control and take action, such as making reasonable assumptions, opening the account, setting up the automatic investments, and making adjustments along the way. That way, you can ignore all of the otherwise worrisome events that are outside your control, such as which party is in control of Congress, the price of oil, and uprisings on other continents. Then, you can achieve your financial goals with a sense of serenity and a lot less worry.

First Accept What Is

To focus on what you can control, it is necessary first to accept what is, i.e., reality. The legendary basketball coach Phil Jackson won six NBA championships coaching the Chicago Bulls and another five coaching the LA Lakers. He was an acknowledged Zen master at this.

In his book, *Sacred Hoops*, he writes:

> In Zen it is said that the gap between accepting things the way they are and wishing them to be otherwise is, "the tenth of an inch of difference between heaven and hell." If we can accept whatever we've been dealt—no matter how unwelcome—the way to proceed eventually becomes clear. This is what is meant by right action: the capacity to observe what's happening and act appropriately, without being distracted by self-centered thoughts. If we rage and resist, our angry, fearful minds have trouble quieting down sufficiently to allow us to act in the most beneficial way for ourselves and others.

Investing Panics and Market Crashes

During the 2020 coronavirus market crash, my business partner, Bob Kargenian, and I spent a lot of time calling clients and explaining how changes in the stock and bond markets affected their accounts. Most of our clients were comforted by these calls and appreciated the updates, especially when we explained that we had temporarily shifted most of their investments into cash. However, some clients tended to worry more than others. Sometimes, that was because they weren't in as strong of a financial position as they would like, but other times, it was just due to their nature.

I spoke with one retired, long-time client at the start of the pandemic, and a few days later, he called me back to let me know he was still worried about the coronavirus and its effect on his investments. I again explained we were positioned very conservatively, and I told him that any further drops in the stock market would have a minimal effect on his accounts. I also reminded him that even after the recent market drop, his account was still well above where it had been 12 months prior, even though he had been taking monthly withdrawals from the account.

I could hear the intense worry in his voice, so I kept asking questions to find out what was really bothering him. He eventually said, "Every channel on TV is talking about the coronavirus 24/7. I can't take it anymore. It's impossible to get away from it."

I would argue that wasn't really true. He could change the channel to something light, or entertaining, or—better still—comedies. Clinical research has shown laughter is measurably the best medicine for your health, and it also reduces stress. Or, he could turn his TV off, but he chose not to. He had decided to focus intently on something out of his control.

Fortunately, our long conversation helped him gain a better perspective and focus on what was within his control. He realized he could temporarily lower his spending or reduce his charitable giving if the market didn't recover soon. He could also choose to turn off the TV and do something more affirming, like taking a walk or giving his dog a belly rub—both proven stress-reducers.

Our conversation reminded me of a story contemporary American author and Buddhist Jack Kornfield often tells:

> I remember once when I was walking with my teacher Ajahn Chah, and he pointed to a boulder in a field and asked, "Is that heavy?" I replied, "Yes, of course." Ajahn Chah smiled and said, "Not if you don't pick it up."

Terry: A Lesson in Reassessing and Pivoting

Terry was born in 1950 and grew up in Southern California. He had an interest in math ever since he was in elementary school. When personal computers became accessible to hobbyists in the 1970s, Terry learned rudimentary programming for fun while completing his college math degree. After that, he got a scholarship to a prestigious out-of-state graduate school, where he completed a master's degree in mathematics. He then worked for 15 years as an operations research analyst for a large energy company, but he found the work way too theoretical and not hands-on enough to be personally fulfilling.

After having had kids and getting divorced at age 43, which he felt was partly due to being so miserable in his career, he decided to make a change. Just as the internet was becoming more accessible in 1993, he opened a business selling custom personal computers. The business boomed as more people were going online, and he had a constant stream of customers. Fortunately, he opened a Simplified Employee Pension (SEP) IRA account and faithfully contributed the maximum, which was 20% of his annual income each year. He also diligently saved outside of his retirement accounts.

From the mid-1990s into the mid-2000s, his business grew, and he had nine employees at the peak. The profitable business allowed him to accumulate significant savings and investments. In 2005, by the age of 55, he was a newly minted millionaire, yet his financial situation was already starting to deteriorate.

Low-cost personal computers were saturating the market-place, which made it impossible to compete on price. As virtually everyone in his market already owned computers by that point, the volume of his computer sales was also dropping. In a slow, agonizing decline, he had to lay off all of his employees and was back to being a one-person shop by 2008.

Terry barely kept his doors open throughout the financial crisis, even though he had much lower overhead costs. It got so bad that his retirement savings came to a halt.

His struggles made him think back to some wisdom he learned growing up from an elderly neighbor named Thomas. Thomas was a successful business owner and impressed upon Terry the importance of focusing on what you can control. When, at age 13, Terry accidentally hit a baseball through Thomas's living room window, he expected him to be furious. Instead, his neighbor calmly surveyed the damage and thanked Terry for having the courage to knock on his door and admit his mistake.

Thomas said, "Terry, what's done is done. There's nothing either of us can do about the window breaking now. But you can help me clean the glass off my floor. I'd also appreciate you finding some cardboard and duct tape to keep the cold air out until the pane can be replaced. Let me know how you and your parents decide to make this right."

Terry gained immense respect for Thomas and eventually learned of his neighbor's interest in ancient Stoic philosophy. Thomas mentored Terry when he faced tough decisions and gave him his worn copy of *Meditations* by Marcus Aurelius. Terry read the book when he was in high school and began rereading it in the 1990s.

The book was a major influence on his decision later in life to start his business. He had felt trapped in his job as an operations research analyst, and he came across this passage in *Meditations*: "The impediment to action advances action. What stands in the way becomes the way." That, among other wisdom in the book, not only helped Terry decide to start his business, it also served him well through each subsequent challenge. The global financial crisis in 2008 reminded him of the lessons he learned growing up: what's done is done. There's nothing anyone can do about the financial crisis itself. All we can do is direct our energy toward improving our situation. And in 2010, he decided to make another change.

Terry shut down his business and began teaching math classes at his local community college to make ends meet. Our meetings around this time were discouraging. Even though he was still technically a millionaire, partly due to the equity in his home, he was dipping into his savings to pay his bills and his mortgage.

A million dollars sounds like a lot of money, but it would only provide $50,000 annual spending for 20 years, without investment gains. Terry was then 60 years old, and the financial projections we ran showed that unless he could turn things around, he would run out of money in his late 70s.

Terry continued to focus on what was within his control when it came to his finances and career. He first concentrated on reducing expenses by eliminating all nonessential spending. This allowed him to live off his teaching income along with minimal withdrawals from his savings.

Next, he focused on increasing his income. He knew his teaching income didn't have the potential to grow much beyond the current level, so he researched other opportunities. As a teacher at the community college, he could audit courses in just about anything that interested him. He gravitated toward computer programming classes because he had so much fun learning the fundamentals in his youth.

When he was taking the classes, he realized Java had replaced C++ as the dominant programming language, and he predicted Java programmers would continue to be in great demand for the foreseeable future. He took Java classes and met Java programmers in the area through his community college connections.

At age 62, he got his first job as a Java software developer while he continued to teach math classes at the college. Even though his income from programming was quite a bit higher than his teaching income and growing, he enjoyed teaching. He liked having the extra income, especially as it was from two independent sources.

Now that Terry was making good money again, it was tempting to allow lifestyle creep to absorb all of his extra income. However, following our discussion, he made a conscious decision to avoid that phenomenon, keep expenses low, and continue paying down his mortgage.

Lifestyle Creep: A Leading Enemy to Reaching Financial Success

Because lifestyle creep is so common, most people are programmed to engage in it subconsciously.

Lifestyle creep is a dynamic in which individuals get a pay raise, meaning they have extra money to spend. Because they worked hard for the pay raise, they sometimes feel compelled to spend all the extra money on the things they want: a car as nice as their neighbors' or a new house in a higher-end neighborhood.

Because they're spending more, they start to live paycheck to paycheck again, so they work even harder to get the next raise, leading to additional stress. The cycle continues to the point that many will soon find themselves running harder but falling further behind, stressed while boosting credit card balances to keep up with their new higher-spending lifestyle. That is not a recipe for financial success or serenity.

Although I do not advocate a life of austerity for my clients, I like to have an objective discussion of how much of that pay increase should augment their lifestyle and how much should be saved toward their financial goals and the peace of mind that brings.

The real point here is to avoid the (media-programmed) human nature to spend any increased income. Anyone serious about financial success or serenity will not find it in the coolest new flat-screen television or a new BMW with 19-inch alloy wheels. And interestingly, once many people realize how good it feels to meet or exceed their financial goals, they become devout savers.

On the other side of Terry's balance sheet, he committed to reinvigorating his savings. Due to his reduced expenses, he was able to maximize his contributions to his company 401(k). Combined with his aftertax savings, he was again saving over 20% of his income each year. Because the market steadily climbed for more than 10 years after the financial crisis, his additional savings grew at a rate higher than the long-term average.

After working as a software developer for seven years, throughout most of his 60s, he fully paid off his home mortgage. Terry's story is an excellent example of spiraling up, where one good decision leads to improved circumstances, which in turn lead to better opportunities.

By making the initial decisions to reduce his expenses and increase his income, Terry created positive monthly cash flow. This positive cash flow allowed him to pay off his mortgage early. With his mortgage payment gone, he had even greater positive cash flow, which gave him better opportunities to invest in income-producing assets and improve his financial situation even more.

Work was optional at that point because his income from his investments and Social Security exceeded his expenses. He decided to stop teaching then, and he also stopped full-time work at his company. However, he still enjoyed the work and decided to continue working part-time for his employer. Now, he works three days per week as a consultant and has the flexibility to set his own hours. More importantly, he has financial abundance and a robust plan as he continues to spiral up.

Summary of Key Points

- The principle of focusing on what you can control has survived for thousands of years. It can help us in every area of our lives, including our finances.

- The other six principles of financial serenity build on the fundamental principle of focusing on what you can control.

- We can control things like our asset allocation and investment choices, keeping investment costs low, and managing our behavior.

- We have some control over our career earnings and duration, as well as our lifespan, based on the choices we make throughout our lives.

- Market returns, politicians, and tax policy are completely out of our control. However, many people spend too much time worrying about those things instead of focusing on the areas where they do have control.

- If you ignore the things outside your control, you'll have more time and energy to focus on the things within your control, like understanding your financial values and taking action to reach your goals.

Terry's Key Lesson

Terry's ability and commitment to focus on what was within his control, especially during the most challenging times that life inevitably brings, is what allowed him to take action that enabled him to move from financial scarcity, through financial security and independence, and into financial serenity.

We can learn a lot from the way that James Stockdale, a POW in Vietnam, and Terry, someone struggling to get in a better financial position, successfully applied the same principle in entirely different circumstances.

While focusing on what he could control was the first principle of Terry's success, he also followed the other principles discussed in the following chapters. He knew intuitively that wealth was a state of mind, and he demonstrated a growth mindset when he went back to school to pursue a second career. Terry understood his personal balance sheet and made it a priority to pay off all his debt. Finally, he developed good financial habits and worked with our firm to develop a plan to build his net worth, balanced with proper risk management.

In the next chapter, we'll explore the second principle of financial serenity: accepting that wealth is a state of mind.

I quote snippets from the ancient teachings of Stoicism, Buddhism, and Zen to illustrate certain principles because they have stood the test of millennia. However, many versions of the same essential philosophy are repackaged in ways that may resonate with you more. I have included a suggested reading list in Appendix B: Recommended Reading for those who would like to explore further.

Chapter 5

Principle Two:
Accept That Wealth Is
a State of Mind

"Thought is the original source of all wealth,
all success, all material gain, all great discoveries and
inventions, and all great achievements."

—**Claude M. Bristol**, *The Magic of Believing*

"Success is commonly defined as money and power,
but increasingly that's not enough. It's almost like
a two-legged stool where you fall over if
that's all you measure your life by."

—**Arianna Huffington**

*"Cultivate the habit of being grateful for every good thing
that comes to you, and to give thanks continuously.
And because all things have contributed to your advancement,
you should include all things in your gratitude."*

—Ralph Waldo Emerson

*"Wealth consists not in having great possessions,
but in having few wants."*

—Epictetus

The Penniless Multimillionaires

Early on a February morning in 1986, Ferdinand and Imelda Marcos, the former president and first lady of the Philippines, were spirited into exile aboard a series of US Air Force helicopters and jets. The People Power Revolution had succeeded in overthrowing the conjugal dictatorship due to rising public discontent with horrific human rights abuses, martial law, and election tampering.

They took a 10-hour flight to Hickam Air Force Base in Hawaii, aboard a US Air Force C-141 Starlifter plane. A second C-141 transport plane carrying the possessions they were able to gather before their escape also accompanied them.

The Guardian later reported that US Customs Service detailed the contents of the 23 wooden crates and various boxes they brought with them. This included: 413 pieces of jewelry, including 70 pairs of jeweled cuff links; 24K gold bricks, engraved, "To my husband on our 24th anniversary"; and stacks of freshly printed Philippine peso notes. US Customs estimated the total value of the contents to be $15 million, which would be worth around $35 million today.

Even after bringing what they could to Hawaii, Imelda famously left behind 15 mink coats, 888 handbags, and 3,000 pairs of shoes in the Malacañang Palace. The Philippines Presidential Commission on Good Government subsequently estimated that Ferdinand and Imelda Marcos looted $5 to $10 *billion* from the Philippine treasury.

Despite their billions of dollars of ill-gotten wealth siphoned out of a poverty-stricken nation and the estimated $15 million of estimated wealth stashed on board the jets, Imelda later described their condition upon their Hawaii arrival as "penniless."

Beware: Your Thoughts Are a Magnet

Her description underscores the reality that wealth or poverty is a state of mind. As Eric Butterworth, the 20th-century theologian, lecturer, and author said, "Prosperity is a way of living and thinking, and not just money or things. Poverty is a way of living and thinking, and not just a lack of money or things." Accepting this timeless concept is a choice, but upon examination, it is difficult to dispute. Once acknowledged, you can cultivate your thoughts accordingly.

By living in a mindset of abundance and gratitude, you draw more wealth to yourself. Unfortunately, the opposite is also true. If you focus on scarcity and what you lack, you will always feel poor, regardless of the balances on your financial statements.

That type of poverty is a self-imposed prison. But before you're too hard on yourself, realize that gravitating toward thoughts of scarcity instead of abundance is not a personal failing—it comes from millennia of evolutionary programming.

Martin Seligman, a University of Pennsylvania professor and the founder of the positive psychology movement, writes in his book, *Flourish*:

> For sound evolutionary reasons, most of us are not nearly as good at dwelling on good events as we are at analyzing bad events. Those of our ancestors who spent a lot of time basking in the sunshine of good events, when they should have been preparing for disaster, did not survive the Ice Age.

The same is true for thoughts of scarcity and abundance, which make it difficult to appreciate what we have unless we overcome our natural tendencies. Fortunately, understanding these tendencies makes it possible to switch from a consciousness of scarcity to one of abundance.

In this chapter, we'll explore some of our beliefs about

money and wealth and different types of irrational behavior resulting from those beliefs. We'll also look at how we can overcome that suboptimal behavior to make better financial decisions. Finally, we'll hear the story of a client who moved from a scarcity to an abundance mindset, and how that transition brought a more significant experience of wealth and joy into her life.

My Head Start to an Abundance Mindset

I feel fortunate that my mom taught me at a young age to be grateful for what we had. When she referred to what we had, she wasn't necessarily talking about toys, our car, or other possessions. She was referring to all the richness of our lives: family, friends, modern technology, and the quality of life we enjoyed compared with our ancestors who lived only a few generations ago. She impressed upon me that if you cannot enjoy a beautiful sunset where you live, you're not going to be any happier jetting off to the French Riviera and watching the sunset there.

As Jon Kabat-Zinn, a PhD in molecular biology from MIT, Zen Buddhist, and prolific contemporary author, said in his book, *Wherever You Go, There You Are*, "If your mind is not centered here, it is likely not to be centered just because you arrive somewhere else." The book focuses on mindfulness and meditation, but his quote is in line with what my mom was saying: if you don't appreciate all the abundance in your life in your present circumstances, winning the lottery will not make you any happier.

It's Normal to Want More

Having said that, extensive research confirms that for most people, feeling rich means wanting more than what one currently has.

The Millionaire Next Door was first published in 1996, and it was revolutionary at the time. Before the book came out, common knowledge suggested that most wealthy people were rich because they were born into wealth. In contrast, the book's authors found that about 80% of millionaires were self-made, based on their 20 years of research. They found that these millionaires became wealthy by following specific rules like spending less than they earn, taking prudent financial risks, avoiding a status lifestyle, and not funding lavish lifestyles for their children.

One of *The Millionaire Next Door* authors, William D. Danko, PhD, coauthored a follow-up book entitled *Richer than a Millionaire: A Pathway to True Prosperity* with Richard J. Van Ness, PhD. In the book, they constructed the graph shown below based on two survey questions.

The first question was about self-reported current net worth, and the responses ranged from $100,000 to over $20 million. The second question was how much the respondent would need to "feel rich." The answers show that whatever someone has, they would need more to feel rich, but the multiplier goes down as wealth increases.

For example, someone who has a net worth of $500,000 would "need" five times as much, or $2.5 million, to feel rich (a 5x multiplier). However, someone with a current net worth of $2.5 million would "need" $5 million to feel rich (a 2x multiplier).

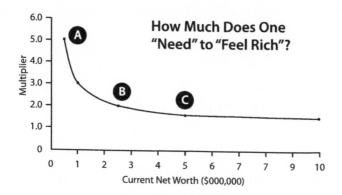

A	If current net worth is $500,000, to "feel rich," one "needs" 5 times as much or $2,500,000.
B	If current net worth is $2,500,000, to "feel rich," one "needs" 2 times as much or $5,000,000.
C	If current net worth is $5,000,000, to "feel rich," one "needs" 1.6 times as much or $8,000,000.

Source: **Richer than a Millionaire: A Pathway to True Prosperity (2017)** *by William D. Danko and Richard J. Van Ness, page 24, used with permission.*

Fortunately, as wealth increases, you may only think you need slightly more to feel rich. But no matter who you are or how successful you've been, it's natural to want more.

That desire is what motivates us to continue to build and grow in our lives, so it's not necessarily a bad thing. This can manifest as earning more money or working hard for a charitable cause instead of retiring to the sofa and television, which would only result in accelerated aging.

If you've been successful but still need to increase your wealth to feel rich, you're not alone. It's okay. But if you want to feel truly wealthy, the first step is acknowledging your reality and examining your beliefs about money.

Our Financial Beliefs

You've probably seen someone who's achieved success and serious monetary wealth, but who still feels terribly poor. They feel like there is never enough, regardless of how much they have. The reasons for this attitude vary, but George Kinder put it well in *The Seven Stages of Money Maturity*: "As soon as we become aware of money, we develop beliefs about it—beliefs we cling to, sometimes for the rest of our lives, often at the cost of our souls."

We all have unconscious beliefs about money typically handed down by parents or otherwise based on associations we made in our formative years. Many of these beliefs, which are unhealthy or counterproductive to our mental, emotional, and physical well-being, are powerfully reinforced by the media, as previously discussed.

It can be extremely challenging to override these beliefs. Although our minds can be marvelously creative at times, they can also be lazy, pattern-seeking machines. If we touch a hot stove as a child, we don't need to be reminded not to touch it again. That association is there for life, and we're not going to question it in the future.

Our associations with money work similarly, but we don't have to accept that an unhelpful association will be there for life. We can work to change those associations.

In *Happy Money: The Japanese Art of Making Peace with Your Money*, author Ken Honda says, "It's those who figure out how to change their attitude toward, and their relationship with, money by healing their past wounds associated with money who seem to feel the wealthiest, regardless of what they have."

So, for example, if we grow up in an environment in which we believe there is never enough, we may develop an unconscious scarcity mindset for the rest of our lives. To an extent, this can be an advantage when it comes to achieving financial security and freedom. It can motivate you to spend less than you earn, save for a rainy day, and invest for the future.

However, the scarcity mindset can also hinder us. There is a point where that virtue becomes a vice. Some people work their entire lives to build their wealth, but they eventually lose the ability to spend it on themselves.

The Multimillionaire
Working for $2.94 per Hour

I know a multimillionaire who regularly drives 15 minutes and four miles out of the way to buy Costco gasoline. The gas is about 20 cents per gallon less expensive than at the local gas station, so filling a 14-gallon gas tank saves about $2.80.

But, is it really a savings if you drive four miles out of your way? Let's do the math. That's eight miles round trip and 30 minutes of your time. Driving eight miles would use one-third of a gallon in a car that gets 24 miles to the gallon. Assuming a gallon costs $4, then one-third of a gallon costs $1.33. This $1.33 gets subtracted from the $2.80 you're saving for a total cash savings of $1.47 (we'll ignore wear and tear on both the car and your nervous system for this discussion).

Is it worth your time to drive 30 minutes out of your way to save $1.47? That's putting a value on your time at $2.94 per hour, less than one-third the hourly wage McDonald's pays its entry-level employees.

This is not to pick on anyone who fills up at Costco; it's a great deal if you're already there. This is simply an example of one of the types of irrational decisions we often make regarding money.

My business partner and I have had meetings where we are practically begging clients to spend their money. They have worked hard for it all their lives, and now they can take that dream cruise or buy the car they've always wanted if those purchases are in accordance with their values.

Sometimes it helps when we convince them that if they don't enjoy their money, their children and the IRS will. In other cases, the money just sits there in their investment accounts until the day they die.

Those who live in financial serenity and abundance are more likely to avoid this trap. Those with an abundance mindset understand it's always possible to generate more money, but you can never create more time. That's why they focus on trading their money for more time (e.g., hiring a home-cleaning or lawn-care service) instead of trading their time for more money (like driving 30 minutes to save $1.47 on Costco gas).

A 2017 study from the US National Academy of Sciences entitled "Buying Time Promotes Happiness" studied large, diverse populations from four continents and concluded that spending money to save time is linked to greater satisfaction in life. Part of that satisfaction comes from the resulting better quality of life, and part comes from the good feeling of providing work and paychecks to those less fortunate than ourselves.

Grateful for the Bill and the
Check You Write

Another issue often accompanying a scarcity mindset is the angst and fatigue that comes with paying bills. If you cringe when you get a bill, you are causing yourself unnecessary worry.

Remember that you made a choice to buy that product or service, and it was presumably at a fair price or you wouldn't have bought it in the first place. You can choose not to purchase it again, but for now, the only choice is to pay the bill. Once you accept that, you can still choose to resent the bill and service provider or simply appreciate that the provider offered a service that you willingly chose.

I recently faced this situation when tree roots found their way into my home's plumbing system. Of course, my first thought was, *I didn't choose to have gray water bubble up from my shower drain and flood my bathroom! That cost me $400, and I don't want to pay it.* I later reflected and realized while I might not have chosen the clogged drain that caused the gray water to bubble up, I did choose to call the plumber. In hindsight, my choice was simple.

One option was to figure out a way to pump the water out myself, along with all the time, cost, and potential water damage that would result from taking so long to figure out how to do the job right. Another option was to live with the water sloshing around my bathroom floor, which would likely lead to worries of toxic mold and a far larger bill to replace the bathroom flooring.

The third and best overall option was to pay $400 to have someone show up and take care of the issue while I could get other work done, sit down and relax, or focus on something else more pleasant. This option eliminated the need to:

✓ Research pumps and drive to a store like Home Depot to rent or purchase equipment
✓ Spend time pumping out the water
✓ Worry about toxic mold
✓ Replace the bathroom flooring

Seen in this light, $400 was a pittance for the service and an option for which I am grateful.

After deciding to call the plumber, I wrote a $400 check, regardless of whether I chose to think about it in a negative or positive light. Choosing the path of resentment would have reinforced worry and the scarcity mindset. However, choosing to appreciate that a service provider showed up on short notice and did everything necessary to prevent further losses strengthened an abundance mindset and feelings of financial serenity.

Shakespeare's Hamlet said, "For there is nothing either good or bad, but thinking makes it so." The choice is ours.

Author Louise Hay's book *You Can Heal Your Life* has sold over 50 million copies. In it, she writes:

It is essential that we stop worrying about money and stop resenting our bills. Many people treat bills as punishments to be avoided if possible. A bill is an acknowledgment of our ability to pay. The creditor assumes you are affluent enough and gives you the service or the product first. I bless with love each and every bill that comes into my home . . . If you pay with resentment, money has a hard time coming back to you. If you pay with love and joy, you open the free-flowing channel of abundance.

Awareness of Our Money Beliefs Is Crucial

We cannot control our experiences with money in our formative years or the associations currently being reinforced through endless media programming. However, we can actively become aware of our associations and determine if they empower or limit us. A limiting belief is something we think to be true but that ultimately constrains us.

If a belief is empowering us, we can continue to support that belief with action. For example, if we make the association that saving a solid portion of our income every month will lead to financial security in the future, we can implement that conviction by setting up an automatic savings and investment plan.

That association may initially serve us well, but it could also constrain us. Suppose it morphs into the limiting belief that spending money on a vacation is an extravagance we can't afford and a frivolous waste of money. In that case, we may never experience the things that could bring us the most happiness in life.

The key is balance. Depending on your income and assets, a first-class air and five-star hotel trip to Paris may indeed be excessive, while an economy ticket and three-star hotel may be well in line. It's still Paris!

The association that saving leads to a better future might allow someone with a moderate income to save over $2 million by the time they retire, which is fantastic. The danger is that the belief about savings can, over time, calcify into a scarcity mindset, in which buying anything beyond the bare necessities is unacceptable. Fortunately, we can decide to change a limiting belief that is not serving us.

Let's take the example of a woman in her 70s who has retirement investment accounts totaling $2.8 million. She got there because she held the empowering belief that diligent saving would lead to future financial security. However, she also developed a limiting belief that her savings are never enough.

Now, she keeps telling herself if she could just get up to the $3 million point, she would feel financially secure. The truth is the dollar amount does not determine her feeling of financial security. When she had less than $2 million in her account, she thought she would feel financially secure by getting to the $2 million level. This is a recipe for endless—and needless—financial and emotional anxiety.

She may decide that spending $25,000 to take her kids and grandkids on a cruise is a frivolous and irresponsible waste of money. Maybe it is—but then again, maybe it isn't. What if that's what she most wants to do with her family, and it's something that will create memories of a lifetime? What if this trip becomes part of family lore for generations and solidifies the familial bonds of all the young cousins, both in childhood and for the rest of their adult lives? If so, it would be unfortunate to miss such an opportunity, especially when $25,000 is a rounding error on any of her monthly investment statements.

If she received her next month-end statement in the mail, and the balance was $2,851,362 instead of $2,876,362, would she even notice the balance is $25,000 less? On any given day, a 1% loss or gain in her accounts would cause the balance to go down or up, respectively, by approximately $28,000.

By examining her limiting belief and reframing her decision, she may well decide to book that cruise and experience all the enjoyment that results directly from her decision and, indirectly, from a lifetime of financial clarity.

How do we overcome these irrational thoughts about money? First, we need to recognize we're not alone. Many people have issues when it comes to their finances.

Next, we need to believe we can change our limiting beliefs. At that point, we need to identify what our limiting beliefs are. Once we recognize that beliefs are just associations we've created in our minds, neither right nor wrong, we can replace limiting beliefs with empowering ones.

For some, that may mean an increased focus on saving and investment while, for others, it may mean enjoying the prosperity already achieved through measured spending, charitable giving, or whatever brings joy and contentment.

Your Financial Belief System:
A Short Exercise of Discovery and Renewal

One simple exercise to examine your belief system about money is to take a blank piece of paper and write down all of your earliest associations with money. Think back to what you heard from your parents and grandparents and write it down. For example, "More money means more problems" or "Rich people are greedy." After you've written down every saying or association you can remember, ask yourself if it's true or not and whether that belief is serving you. Finally, come up with an empowering belief to replace your limiting belief.

The idea that more money means more problems may be at least partly true. Over two thousand years ago, the Greek philosopher Epicurus said, "The acquisition of riches has been for many men, not an end, but a change, of troubles."

But that alone is not a reason to shun wealth. True or not, is that belief serving you or sabotaging your wealth mindset? If it's not serving you, replace it with a more empowering belief like, "Having more money may result in new challenges, but it will give me better quality challenges as well as more options and opportunities throughout my life."

If you have a belief that rich people are greedy, ask yourself first if that's true. Yes, some rich people are greedy, but many are exceedingly generous. Look to The Giving Pledge, a campaign to inspire the wealthiest people in the world to donate half of their net worth to philanthropic causes.

Bill Gates and Warren Buffett began recruiting members 10 years ago, and to date, over $1.2 trillion has been pledged. Given the generosity of so many billionaires and millionaires, a more empowering belief may be, "*Some* rich people are greedy, but *I* will join those who generously use their wealth to make the world a better place."

As with everything in life, there is a balance. My intention is not to project my financial values on anyone else. But understanding that wealth is a state of mind will hopefully help you see through some of your limiting unconscious beliefs, gain a better understanding of what fulfills you, and take action to ensure that your values and your actions are aligned.

Barbara: A 55-Year Journey to a Wealth Mindset

Barbara is 89 years of age and has a wealth mindset, but it wasn't always that way. She had a career as a nurse, and her husband was a general contractor. After he died in a tragic slip-and-fall accident, Barbara became a single mother raising their four kids, who were 6, 8, 11, and 13 years old at the time. Barbara was only 34, and, unfortunately, they did not have life insurance.

With her modest income and all of the costs of raising children, Barbara always struggled to make ends meet. While she wasn't able to give her kids everything they wanted financially, she scrimped and saved and provided her family the necessities.

Barbara developed impressive saving and spending habits, and she honed them almost to the point of becoming a miser. She used the envelope budgeting method to set aside what she needed for bills and savings every month. She'd divide her expenses into different categories like utilities, groceries, entertainment, etc. After deciding how much she'd need for each type of expense, that amount of money would go into a separate envelope for each category. She turned coupon cutting into an art, enlisting her kids to scour the newspaper inserts for the best weekly deals.

Even though money was tight, she always invested in her hospital retirement savings plan, at least up to the point that her employer matched her contributions. Her plan allowed saving money for retirement on a tax-deferred basis. As her kids left home over the years, her expenses went down, but she didn't increase her spending. Instead, she expanded her savings and refined her budgeting skills over three decades.

When she first met my business partner 25 years ago at age 64, her primary goal was to see if she had saved enough money to retire from nursing. She had managed to completely pay off her home and a condo she purchased as a rental property. The rental property was providing about $2,000 per month of income after expenses.

She had also saved about $450,000 in her hospital retirement plan. Using a withdrawal rate of 4%, we calculated that she could withdraw $18,000 per year from the account, or $1,500 per month, to supplement her income in retirement.

However, she didn't need to take an income from her investments. Because she had no mortgage payment and had cultivated her habit of saving instead of spending, her expenses remained very low. Her $2,000 monthly rental income, when combined with her $2,100 Social Security benefit, was more than enough to meet her monthly expenses. We rolled over her hospital retirement plan into an IRA account, and she retired at age 64.

For the next 13 years after she retired, Barbara didn't touch her IRA account other than withdrawing her required minimum distributions (RMDs). Her IRA account grew from $450,000 to $720,000 during that period, and at age 77, she still didn't need the money. Her expenses were already covered because her rental income and Social Security income increased with inflation, and Barbara continued to keep her expenses low. Even though she was required to take out her RMD each year, she just took the money out of her IRA and put it right back into her savings.

Then when Barbara was 78 years old, tragedy struck again.

She lost her 57-year-old son, her oldest child, to heart disease. That's when her outlook on life began to change. She read every book she could find on nutrition, exercise, sleep, and meditation—what she called "the four pillars of health." At age 78, she made positive changes to her lifestyle in all four of those areas. She began taking yoga and meditation classes. She also studied art and started making pottery.

But the biggest change was in her mindset about wealth and what wealth meant to her. Her meditation teacher taught her that living in a state of gratitude was the source of her wealth, not a dollar amount. When she accepted that, she truly began to live in abundance. She had always viewed life through the scarcity lens, but she started to realize she had more money than she could realistically spend in her remaining years.

She also read a quote from Oprah Winfrey that struck a chord with her: "Be thankful for what you have; you'll end up having more. If you concentrate on what you don't have, you will never, ever have enough." That's what led her from not just living in abundance, but to also feeling gratitude for all that she had.

From her yoga teacher, she learned the Buddhist proverb, "Serenity comes when you trade expectations for acceptance." While she certainly did not choose or expect the loss of her husband or her son, she was able to accept the losses with time. Her acceptance led to a slight sense of tranquility. Once she began to internalize these feelings of abundance, gratitude, and tranquility, she was on the path to financial serenity.

After reaching that level of awareness, she realized she could spend her money on what was important to her without feeling guilt. Instead of just moving her required IRA account withdrawals into savings each year, she began to help her children and grandchildren financially.

She also donated money to the American Heart Association, hoping their work could help prevent deaths like her son's. Our meetings shifted from merely making sure she wouldn't run out of money to making sure she had the cash flow to gift her money to the people and organizations most important in her life.

At 89, Barbara remains one of our most optimistic and spirited clients, even though she's started to have some health challenges in recent years. She is mindfully allocating her money and time in alignment with her values and joys. With appreciation for all that she has, Barbara is a shining example of one who has accepted that wealth is a state of mind.

A Tool to Increase Gratitude

It's scientifically proven that writing about things for which you are grateful increases feelings of gratitude. *The Sunrise Manifesto*, a guided morning journal, is designed to take less than five minutes each morning. The journal has several daily prompts, but the ones most relevant to increasing gratitude are as follows:

- Three things I am grateful for:
  - Something I earned or was given: _____.
  - A person or relationship: _____.
  - Something simple: _____.
- Something from yesterday that makes me smile when I think about it: _____.

Excerpt from *The Sunrise Manifesto Guided Morning Journal*, used with permission.

Summary of Key Points

- Either wealth or poverty is a state of mind.
- You can choose to accept that wealth is a state of mind and cultivate your thoughts accordingly.
- If you live in abundance and gratitude, you not only feel wealthy, you attract more wealth.
- The opposite is also true. If you focus on what you don't have, you will always feel poor, even if you're objectively well-off. A scarcity consciousness repels people and opportunities, while an abundance consciousness naturally draws them to you.
- No matter how wealthy you become, it's natural to want more in life, which can be a good thing. But feeling

genuinely wealthy requires that you first acknowledge that fact and examine your beliefs about money.

- Many of our money beliefs are handed down by parents or are created by making associations in childhood. Left unquestioned, this can lead to irrational and counter-productive financial behavior. By examining these limiting beliefs, we can replace them with new empowering beliefs.

- By exploring our values, we can channel our money and energy toward the things that are most important to us. This reduces our irrational decisions and increases our wealth.

A Study of Opposites

We opened this chapter with the story of a fabulously wealthy person who thought of herself as penniless and closed with the story of someone of comparatively modest means who lives in wealth and abundance.

In the next chapter, we'll discuss how another facet of our thoughts, having a growth mindset, is indispensable in the quest to spiral up financially.

Chapter 6

Principle Three: Cultivate a Growth Mindset

"True self-confidence is 'the courage to be open—
to welcome change and new ideas regardless of their source.'
Real self-confidence is not reflected in a title, an expensive suit,
a fancy car, or a series of acquisitions. It is reflected
in your mindset: your readiness to grow."

—**Carol S. Dweck**, *Mindset: The New Psychology of Success*

"Everything can be taken from a man but one thing:
the last of the human freedoms—to choose one's attitude in any
given set of circumstances, to choose one's own way."

—**Viktor E. Frankl**, *Man's Search for Meaning*

"Learning is the beginning of wealth."

"Formal education will make you a living;
self-education will make you a fortune."

—Jim Rohn

"The way of success is the way of continuous
pursuit of knowledge."

—Napoleon Hill, *Think and Grow Rich*

The Best College Basketball
Coach in History

Bill Walton was a top-recruited college basketball player in 1970 and accepted a scholarship at national powerhouse UCLA. He was excited to get started in his first practice, as were the other star recruits and returning members of the UCLA national championship team.

His first practice started with their coach, John Wooden, saying, "Men, this is how you put your shoes and socks on." He went on to demonstrate, in meticulous detail, how to pull the socks tight and eliminate wrinkles, then showed the method to snugly and completely lace and tie their basketball shoes.

Walton couldn't believe what he was hearing. He rejected the idea that such talented players needed this basic advice. As he recounted in his autobiography, "We were stunned. We looked around and at each other. Are you kidding me? We're all high school All-American players and here is this silly little old man showing us how to put on our shoes and socks!"

However, Walton and other elite UCLA players like Kareem Abdul-Jabbar would all eventually come to understand that continuously learning ways to improve was one of the keys to their coach's success. Wooden knew the team could only be at its best if everyone was ready to play. Properly putting on their shoes and socks meant never getting blisters that would prevent them from hitting the court.

Wooden won 10 NCAA basketball championships in 12 years, including a record seven national titles in a row. He's widely regarded as the best college basketball coach of all time, and he is arguably the best coach of any sport in American history.

One thing that set him apart reinforces the ideas put forth in Principle One: Coach Wooden taught his players to focus on what they could control.

In his book, *Wooden: A Lifetime of Observations and Reflections On and Off the Court*, he wrote, "Too often we get distracted by what is outside our control. You can't do anything about yesterday. The door to the past has been shut and the key thrown away. You can do nothing about tomorrow. It is yet to come. However, tomorrow is in large part determined by what you do today. So, make today a masterpiece. You have control over that."

But the coach didn't stop there. He is also known for something called "a growth mindset." In a growth mindset, individuals trust that they can develop their most basic abilities through hard work and dedication. This is the opposite of a fixed mindset, which says individuals cannot improve their abilities, despite diligent efforts.

Carol Dweck, PhD, a preeminent psychology professor at Stanford University, observed over 30 years ago that some students froze after setbacks while others rebounded quickly. She coined the terms "fixed mindset" and "growth mindset" to describe the students' underlying beliefs about learning a new skill.

Those with a fixed mindset thought that they were born with a certain amount of intelligence, and their grades were simply a reflection of that. On the other hand, those with a growth mindset believed they could get smarter with effort, which led them to put in extra time studying, leading to higher achievement and better outcomes.

Fixed and growth mindsets don't just apply to academic pursuits; they are also relevant in other areas of life, including sports and finances.

In Professor Dweck's book, *Mindset: The New Psychology of Success*, which sold over two million copies, she writes:

> Wooden is not complicated. He's wise and interesting, but not complicated. He's just a straight-ahead growth-mindset guy who lives by this rule: "You have to apply yourself each day to become a little better. By applying yourself to the task of becoming a little better each and every day over a period of time, you will become a lot better."

Putting shoes and socks on properly was just one small example of teaching his players how they could continuously learn new skills to get a lot better over time.

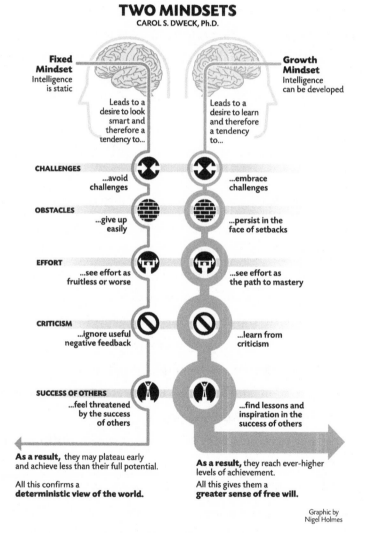

TWO MINDSETS
CAROL S. DWECK, Ph.D.

Fixed Mindset
Intelligence is static

Leads to a desire to look smart and therefore a tendency to...

Growth Mindset
Intelligence can be developed

Leads to a desire to learn and therefore a tendency to...

CHALLENGES
...avoid challenges

...embrace challenges

OBSTACLES
...give up easily

...persist in the face of setbacks

EFFORT
...see effort as fruitless or worse

...see effort as the path to mastery

CRITICISM
...ignore useful negative feedback

...learn from criticism

SUCCESS OF OTHERS
...feel threatened by the success of others

...find lessons and inspiration in the success of others

As a result, they may plateau early and achieve less than their full potential.

All this confirms a **deterministic view of the world.**

As a result, they reach ever-higher levels of achievement.

All this gives them a **greater sense of free will.**

Graphic by Nigel Holmes

Source: Nigel Holmes, used with permission.

These ideas are essential for financial success. Those who throw their hands up and say, "I'm just not good with money," will always struggle with their finances, no matter how much money they have.

Those who realize that managing their finances is a skill they can improve are in a much stronger position. They can then decide to develop their abilities, and this leads to better financial outcomes.

Developing New Financial Skills

In *Man's Search for Meaning*, prominent 20th-century psychiatrist, neurologist, and Holocaust survivor Viktor E. Frankl said, "When we are no longer able to change a situation, we are challenged to change ourselves." We cannot change what is happening in the economy, but we can develop our capabilities and change our actions regarding our finances.

We can decide to learn sound financial skills and to put our knowledge into action. For example, if our tax rate increases, we can learn about and open up a tax-deferred account like an IRA to keep more of what we earn.

One way to build financial skills is through reading time-tested books. Not everything in these books will apply to you, but the relevant wisdom can help you avoid mistakes and develop valuable new expertise. I've listed some of my favorite books on topics ranging from finance to psychology to personal growth in Appendix B: Recommended Reading.

Another way to learn new strategies is by talking with credible people. Sometimes friends or relatives can be credible, but be cautious about who you ask for financial advice. If that person's finances are a mess, it's unlikely they're going to be able to give you good advice. In 1926, George Clason wrote in *The Richest Man in Babylon*, "Advice is one thing that is freely given away, but watch that you only take what is worth having."

Trusted advisors who earn their living giving fiduciary advice can also be great resources to help you cultivate advanced financial literacy. A fiduciary is legally bound to give you the duties of good faith and trust (more details are available in Appendix C: Selecting a Financial Planner). The advantage of working with a trusted advisor is that they know your specific circumstances and can help you develop the most relevant knowledge to accomplish what is most important to you.

For instance, if you have a goal to retire by age 60, a competent planner can review your entire financial situation and teach you the pros and cons of the various retirement savings strategies available to you. Then, you can jointly create and implement a plan to increase your savings and build up your nest egg to where it needs to be by age 60.

In all of the above situations, a growth mindset is the foundation for improving your finances. Having a growth mindset is understanding that even though you don't know the answer yet, you know you can figure it out—or can find an expert who can.

Marie Forleo couldn't have said it better in her outstanding book, *Everything Is Figureoutable*:

> What stops you is never external. Ever. It's never about the lack of money or time or anything else. It's about your internal game, your commitment to do whatever it takes to be creative, get resourceful, and figure it out. To find or make a way ahead, no matter what.
>
> This recognition is the key to a growth mindset, and it will open countless doors, financial and otherwise.

The Growth Mindset Path Forward

Step One

Commit to learning new financial skills. This is the first step in going from where you are financially to where you want to go. The good news is by reading this book, you have already shown your commitment.

Step Two

Define specifically what you want in your financial life. The best way to do that is to write down a detailed description of your ideal financial future. Something magical happens when you commit pen to paper and write down what you want. It's much more potent than just dreaming or thinking about it. Writing down your exact goals sets the wheels in motion and sets the stage for accomplishing those goals.

You can do this on a computer, though I always recommend writing goals like this out by hand. Writing by hand has been linked to improved creativity, and it also improves the biological process of encoding, which happens when the hippocampus analyzes what we perceive and causes the brain to dispose of some pieces of information while storing others in long-term memory. Since writing by hand improves encoding, your thoughts are more likely to be remembered for the long term.

Writing your thoughts down is also essential because simply saying, "I want to be rich," is not enough to set the wheels in motion. However, explicitly defining what you want in life doesn't have to be overly long or complicated.

When I was a 24-year-old US Navy submarine officer in Pearl Harbor, Hawaii, I went through this exercise and wrote out my goals in a straightforward bullet point format. I wrote down things like "graduate from a top-tier MBA program," "travel all over the world," and "learn to speak conversational Spanish." There were about a dozen goals on the list, ranging from financial to professional to personal.

Back then, I had no realistic way of accomplishing the goals because I didn't have the necessary time, money, or other resources. I put the notebook in a drawer somewhere and eventually forgot about it. When my tour of duty in Hawaii ended, I packed up my notebook along with my other belongings, and it sat in a storage box for the next several years, a period when I finished my navy tour in San Francisco then moved to Philadelphia to attend Wharton's MBA program.

After graduating from business school, I moved back to Orange County, California, where I had grown up. When I was unpacking the boxes in my new home, I came across the notebook and the goals I had written eight years earlier. I had not consciously thought about the goals in all those years, so I was amazed that I had accomplished every single thing on the list.

The point is not that I checked off some goals. It's that even though I had no realistic way of accomplishing the goals when I wrote them down, I still accomplished them because I was committed to learning new skills, being resourceful, and figuring it out.

That's the essence of having a growth mindset. It's having the belief that even though you don't know how you're going to achieve what you want, you know you'll be able to learn the skills required to do so.

Whether you write your goals in bullet point format or in a few short paragraphs, you can capture the basics of what you're working toward in just 10 or 15 minutes. What matters most is that you are specific and that you write your goals down—just thinking about them is not enough.

It's also a good idea to revisit and edit your goals as time passes. If I had known how powerful this technique is, I probably would have done so myself. The fact I had forgotten what I had written down for eight years and was so surprised later to see what I had accomplished is what made me believe in the power of this exercise.

I have a colleague who has had the habit of writing her goals down for many years. We once were talking about it with another colleague, and she said, "At this point, as soon as I write something down, it practically just happens. I don't know why it works, but I know it does."

She wasn't bragging. She was as surprised as I was about the power of this method and just wanted to share. It may not have been quite as simple as she said, but by writing down her goals and having the core belief that she'd be able to learn what was required to accomplish them, she did just that.

Step Three

To effectively achieve your goals, you also have to believe you have agency, or the capacity to exert power over your destiny. In the 1937 classic *Think and Grow Rich*, Napoleon Hill says, "You are the master of your destiny. You can influence, direct and control your own environment. You can make your life what you want it to be."

This belief is a central component to the growth mindset because it will give you the fuel to make necessary changes.

Without making changes, you'll continue to get what you've always gotten in the past. Or, as the Chinese philosopher Lao Tzu said over two thousand years ago, "If you do not change direction, you might end up where you are heading."

Step Four

After committing to a growth mindset, describing your ideal financial future, and trusting that you have agency, the next step is to develop a plan to get there. Write down the specific steps you will take today, this week, this month, and this year to get closer to your goals. It's not necessary or productive to try to tackle all your goals at the same time. It's okay to start small.

For example, an excellent initial goal might be to save three to six months' worth of living expenses in your emergency fund. This can be a great place to start as it's easy to track your progress. Developing the plan also underscores the need to build effective financial habits, which we will discuss in Principle Six: Develop Good Financial Habits.

As you accomplish smaller goals that reinforce your growth mindset, your ability and commitment to achieving your more complicated goals will naturally follow, yet another way of spiraling up. If the person who used to say they're "just not good with money" adopts a growth mindset, they can become financially skilled by investing their time and attention into doing exactly that.

Jen and Christopher: Spiraling Up through a Growth Mindset

Jen and Christopher are both Gen Xers in their late 40s.

Jen's Story

Jen was born in a suburb of San Diego in the mid-1970s and grew up in a family where finances were not discussed or understood. There was never enough money to go around, so Jen figured out ways to get creative at a young age.

When she was still in elementary school, she would pick lemons off her backyard tree and make lemonade for a makeshift stand she set up in front of her home. She learned if she set a basket of lemons next to the stand, she could sell lemons for 10 cents each when the neighbors bought a cup of lemonade. This helped her see early in life that she could improve her circumstances through her own efforts and perseverance. Although she had dreams of college, her parents told her it wasn't an option.

Her parents convinced her to join the US Air Force because it offered a steady paycheck, and her uncle had retired with an Air Force pension. She enlisted at age 17 and trained in aircraft electrical systems. She served for four years until age 21, but living at the remote Vance Air Force Base in Oklahoma and the prospect of moving to a new base every few years wasn't for her.

Jen left the USAF and began working as a receptionist in an electronics company in Orange County, California. Even though nobody in her family had graduated from college, she believed she could accomplish anything she set her mind to through hard work, including earning a college degree. She lived with her brother to reduce her expenses, which allowed her to pay for community college. Jen was able to complete her AA degree in three years, even though she was working full-time.

Then she transferred to California State University, Fullerton, and finished her degree four years later, in her late 20s. She was so focused on getting the right classes and earning her degree while working 40 hours per week that she never had the time or energy to learn how student loans work. Instead, she used her credit cards and paid exorbitantly high interest rates without realizing how that was a constant drain on her finances.

Jen graduated with $18,000 of credit card debt at 20% interest. That meant she was paying $3,600 of interest charges every year. She was paying the minimum each month, so she was treading water and not making any progress toward paying off the debt.

Finishing her degree eventually allowed her to move from reception into a technical sales role in the electronics company. After proving herself in sales, she worked as a sales manager for the firm, and her income steadily increased. Although she was paying $300 every month on her credit cards, she noticed the balance wasn't going down. She resolved to understand how the cards worked and to put herself in a stronger financial position.

Jen researched the topic online and found that paying $300 per month toward interest meant all of that money she sent was just going to the credit card company, and none of it was paying down the principal of her debt. She was infuriated and tired of being in debt, so she decided then and there to get control of her finances. Her growth mindset shaped her thoughts: even though her knowledge about money was limited, she would figure it out.

Christopher's Story

Jen's future husband, Christopher, was born in Los Angeles in the early-1970s. Growing up, he was tall for his age, which was a big advantage in volleyball, his favorite sport. He was an excellent player until high school. That's when other players started catching up to him in height, and he slowly turned into an average player. He had never been so frustrated as when he didn't make the varsity team and his best friend did.

His friend was only average height, but he made up for his lack of size with an intense dedication toward the sport. In every practice, his friend was laser focused on what the coach said. He'd walk to and from school every day bumping and setting a volleyball, much to the amusement and sometimes ridicule of the other students.

His friend's success helped instill the belief in Christopher that the best volleyball players weren't just born with some supernatural gift; their talent was the result of hard work. His height had helped him when he was younger, but that advantage was gone now that he was only slightly taller than the average player. That's when he rededicated himself to learning the fundamentals of the sport and improving his skills through focused, deliberate practice. Christopher made the varsity team the following year and was able to get a partial college volleyball scholarship.

He studied engineering in college then worked at a multinational engineering firm in Los Angeles for a few years. He found he spent much of his time doing repetitive, routine tasks that didn't intellectually stimulate him, so he researched other career paths. A chance meeting with one of his college classmates, who had graduated from law school, got him interested in pursuing a law degree and applying his engineering knowledge to the legal profession.

Christopher was accepted at a top law school in Chicago. He left his engineering job and received his law degree after three challenging years there. He took a job with a law firm in Orange County specializing in intellectual property law. In his new role, he protected his clients' proprietary engineering designs, processes, and inventions from competitors who were trying to overcome his clients' market advantage.

He found he enjoyed the intellectual challenges of fusing his technical engineering knowledge with his newly acquired legal expertise. The good news was that he was now earning more than ever before—the bad news was he had spent down most of his savings and racked up over $150,000 in student loan debt during his years in law school.

Jen and Christopher's Combined Finances

When Christopher and Jen began dating, they were both struggling financially and had a combined net worth in negative territory, meaning they had more debt than assets. However, their human capital was off the charts, which meant they now had education, skills, and significant earning potential in their respective careers. They had both made it through some lean years but now had brighter prospects for the future.

Jen was in her sales management role and slowly chipping away at her credit card debt. Christopher was able to pay down small chunks of his student loan debt because he kept his expenses low. This continued for a couple of years while they were dating, but they knew if they ever wanted to buy a home and be able to afford to have kids, they would need to make some significant changes.

After they got engaged, they made a mutual commitment to learn about and improve their finances. First, they decided to work with a reputable nonprofit credit counseling service. They spoke with a debt coach, who worked with them to develop a debt management plan. They then committed to aggressively paying down Jen's high-interest-rate credit card debt first and only making the minimum payments on Christopher's student loan debt as that was at a much lower interest rate.

After they were married, they used their surplus income to pay off her credit card debt completely. Once the credit card debt was gone, their monthly cash flow improved, allowing them to put more money toward Christopher's student loan debt (this is called the debt avalanche strategy, and we'll look at it in more detail in Principle Five: Use Debt Wisely, and Pay It Off).

At the same time, they began saving toward retirement in their company 401(k) plans. At first, they could only save up to the amount of their respective companies' match, which was 4% of Jen's salary and 3% of Christopher's. As they paid down his remaining student loan debt and their incomes increased, they were able to contribute more to each of their retirement plans.

By the time they came to our firm for help, five years into their marriage, they were earning more income than they ever had. In fact, their federal and state income tax bill was now greater than their combined *income* was when they got engaged. That meant they had to learn new strategies to minimize their tax bill and keep more of what they earned.

We showed them how maximizing contributions into their 401(k) plans would reduce their taxable income. They also bought a home to take advantage of the mortgage interest deduction, opened a health savings account (HSA) to reduce taxable income, and opened 529 accounts as soon as their sons were born to save for college on a tax-advantaged basis.

All of this was done in conjunction with developing the right investment strategy for them and ensuring they had the proper amount of insurance coverage.

We also made sure that they had an appropriate estate plan. In the most basic sense, their estate plan outlined what would happen to all their assets if they were to pass away unexpectedly: who would receive their assets, what they would receive, and when they would receive it. The estate plan also allowed them to minimize legal fees and court costs. In addition, the plan named a guardian for their minor children, gave instructions for their care if they became incapacitated, and outlined other details that would be important in the case of their unexpected death.

These changes put Jen and Christopher in a healthier position and allowed them to focus on their family and careers instead of worrying about their finances. Their growth mindset resulted in making better decisions, which led to the improved circumstances and opportunities that further elevated their financial situation.

Summary of Key Points

- Having a fixed mindset means believing an individual is naturally good or bad at something based on their inherent qualities. For example, "She's a natural at managing money" or "He's just not good with finances."

- Having a growth mindset means believing an individual can improve at something over time by dedicating effort and energy. For example, "Even though he didn't learn anything about saving or investing while growing up, his commitment to studying personal finance has helped him become very wealthy over time."
- Because most of us are never taught the basics of personal finance, having a growth mindset is essential for financial success. Those who realize that managing their finances is a skill can then decide to develop their abilities, leading to better outcomes.
- Steps to Implement a Growth Mindset with Your Finances
  - Step One: Recognize the benefits of a growth mindset and commit to learning new financial skills.
  - Step Two: Define specifically what you want in your financial life by writing out a detailed description of your ideal financial future and goals.
  - Step Three: To achieve your goals, you also have to believe you have agency, the capacity to exert influence over your destiny.
  - Step Four: After committing to a growth mindset, describing your ideal financial future, and trusting that you have agency, the last step is to develop a plan to get there.

The Broader Lesson

A growth mindset was essential for Jen and Christopher's financial success, and that is true for all of us. The specific strategies that applied to them may be different for another family, but tax laws, the economy, and particular strategies change over time. The broader lesson is that even though finance skills didn't come easily to them, adopting a growth mindset allowed them to believe they could learn and apply their knowledge to put themselves in a more robust situation for the future.

Jen and Christopher started from a place of financial scarcity, but they began moving toward financial security after they met. Their continued willingness to learn and apply new financial strategies has put them on a path toward financial independence, financial freedom, and ultimately, financial serenity.

Their mindset was similar to Coach John Wooden's, whose secret of success was teaching his players how they could get better by ceaseless learning and focused effort. He cultivated the process of becoming an outstanding player rather than relying on natural talent.

The same is true regarding your finances. You may not think of yourself as being gifted in that area, but you can cultivate financial expertise with a growth mindset. Once you believe that, you can begin to develop financial skills, including knowing how to control your main financial levers. Those levers are in your personal financial statement, and that is the topic of our next chapter.

Chapter 7

Principle Four:
Understand Your Personal
Financial Statement

"Financial literacy begins by understanding
your personal financial statement. The reality is
that money doesn't make you rich. What does make you rich
is your financial IQ. Give the same $100,000 to a person
with a low financial IQ and a person with a high financial
IQ and I guarantee you'll see a vast difference
in how that money is spent and grown."

—**Robert Kiyosaki**, author on personal finance with
over 41 million books sold in 51 languages

A Fundamental Lack of
Financial Literacy

In 2017, Johnny Depp, the actor who starred as Captain Jack Sparrow in *Pirates of the Caribbean*, sued his former financial advisors for $25 million, alleging fraud and negligence. His former advisors promptly filed a counter lawsuit alleging that Depp created his financial problems all by himself.

The advisors' attorney said, "Johnny Depp alone was solely responsible for his extravagant spending. Over 17 years, The Management Group did everything possible to protect the actor from himself."

The advisors alleged that Depp, who was then 53, would often spend more than $2 million per month, despite their warnings that he was spending too fast. The countersuit also said he spent over $75 million buying 14 properties, including a French château and a four-island chain in the Bahamas, and that he bought so much art and Hollywood memorabilia that housing it required 12 storage facilities.

The parties eventually settled the lawsuits for an undisclosed amount in 2018 before they ever went to trial, so we may never know how much Depp was at fault or if his advisors were partly to blame.

What we do know is that Depp had earned approximately $650 million in his career, and by the time of the lawsuit, almost all of it was gone.

According to *Vanity Fair*, Depp said, "I'm not a lawyer. I'm not an accountant. I'm not qualified to help my 15-year-old son with his math homework . . . I've always trusted the people around me." While that all may be true, he still had a responsibility to understand the basics of his own personal finances.

This unfortunate story is an admittedly extreme example of someone imploding because they didn't understand financial basics. Still, the lessons for those of us with far fewer assets remain every bit as valid.

To identify how Depp could have prevented his personal financial crisis, we'll first need to understand the fundamentals of personal financial statements. Then we can take these concepts and apply them to your finances.

Financial success is less about investing knowledge and more about your behavior. However, choosing the right behaviors depends on understanding the four main levers that control virtually everything in your financial life. These levers are your income, expenses, assets, and liabilities, and they are all contained in your personal financial statement. This might initially sound complex, but it is simpler than you think.

Financial Literacy Doesn't Need
to Be Complicated

When I was studying finance in Wharton's MBA program, one of the most challenging courses was corporate accounting. As a former engineer, I wasn't intimidated when other students told me how complex accounting would be—that was, until I actually started the course. It was one of my most difficult classes, and I barely got through it.

In that course, I did learn how to read a corporate income statement and balance sheet. However, I never fully appreciated how one affects the other. I didn't entirely understand these concepts until I moved away from corporate finance and began to study personal finance in depth. Only after years of studying personal finance did I appreciate the importance of the interplay between the four primary financial levers: income, expenses, assets, and liabilities.

Again, this may sound complicated. It took me years to master these concepts, but the good news is genuine mastery is not necessary. All you need is a working knowledge. Even without any formal financial education, understanding the basics of a personal financial statement is well within the grasp of anyone willing to invest the time.

It's actually quite simple once you understand how income and expenses affect assets and debts (and vice versa). The first step is to understand what makes up your personal financial statement.

This statement includes two documents. First is your personal balance sheet; second is your personal income statement. We'll start by defining what these mean in simplified terms, but first, a note on taxes: given that this chapter's purpose is to gain a working knowledge of assets, liabilities, income, and expenses, we'll largely ignore taxes to keep the examples as easy to understand as possible.

Personal Balance Sheet

Your personal balance sheet gives you an overall snapshot of your wealth at a given moment in time. It summarizes what you own (assets) along with what you owe (debts). Debts are also known as liabilities, and I'll use the two terms interchangeably in this book. These two items offset to determine your net worth, which is simply assets minus liabilities:

Balance Sheet	
Assets—things you own that ideally produce income and increase in value (stocks, bonds, real estate). Assets also include things you own that lose value or depreciate, such as cars, boats, jacuzzis, televisions, clothing, and household appliances.	Liabilities—money you owe that results from borrowing money today to buy something you can't otherwise afford. The borrowed money has to be repaid with interest at a later date. A home mortgage and student loans are typical examples, but so are automobile and credit card loans.
	Net Worth = Assets - Liabilities

Net worth results from subtracting your debts from your assets. In the example below, if someone owns a house worth $900,000 and has an investment portfolio of $500,000 but they owe $300,000 on their home mortgage, they would have a net worth of $1.1 million ($900,000 home + $500,000 investment portfolio − $300,000 debt = $1.1 million net worth).

Balance Sheet – Example December 31, 20__			
Assets		**Liabilities**	
Home	$900,000	Home Mortgage	$300,000
Investment Portfolio	$500,000	**Total Liabilities**	$300,000
Total Assets	**$1,400,000**	Net Worth = (Assets − Liabilities)	**$1,100,000**

Personal Income Statement

A personal income statement (also known as a personal cash flow statement) is a document that allows you to keep track of your monthly income sources and expenses at a glance.

Income Statement
Income—money you receive, generally on a regular basis, from work you perform or investments you own.
Expenses—money spent on things like food, housing costs, insurance, entertainment, travel, education, etc.
Net Income = Income – Expenses

This document determines your net income (also called net cash flow) over a certain period, like a month or a year. This is simply the result of subtracting your expenses from your income during that period. This number is crucial because it determines whether you can invest in income-producing assets or will be forced to cut expenses—or borrow money to make ends meet, resulting in going further into debt.

For example, if someone has an annual aftertax income of $100,000 and annual expenses of $95,000, they have a positive net cash flow of $5,000 per year. That $5,000 can be spent on material goods, services, or experiences. Alternatively, it can be used to purchase income-producing assets, pay down debt, or invest in things such as that person's education or a small business.

A Tale of Two Families

Let's look at simplified personal financial statements of two hypothetical millionaire families—the Smiths and the Joneses. You'll notice both families have salaries of $200,000 per year, and both families have a net worth of $1.5 million.

However, that's where the similarities end. Take a look at the personal financial statements for both families below, and we'll dive into what makes them so different.

Personal Financial Statement
—Smith Family

Balance Sheet – Smith Family December 31, 20__			
Assets		**Liabilities**	
Home	$800,000	Home Mortgage	$410,000
Rental Condo	$500,000	Condo Mortgage	$200,000
Investment Portfolio	$700,000	Car Loans	$0
Cars (2)	$60,000	Credit Cards	$0
Emergency Fund	$50,000	**Total Liabilities**	**$610,000**
Total Assets	**$2,110,000**	Net Worth = (Assets – Liabilities)	**$1,500,000**

Income Statement – Smith Family For Year Ending December 31, 20__	
Income	
Salary	$200,000
Rental Property	$24,000
Investment Portfolio Income	$28,000
Total Income	**$252,000**
Expenses	
Home Mortgage	$35,000
Condo Mortgage	$15,000
Condo Expenses	$5,000
Living Expenses	$165,000
Total Expenses	**$220,000**
Net Income = (Income – Expenses)	**$32,000**

Personal Financial Statement
—Jones Family

Balance Sheet – Jones Family December 31, 20__			
Assets		**Liabilities**	
Home	$1,200,000	Home Mortgage	$350,000
Investment Portfolio	$600,000	Car Loans	$80,000
Cars (2)	$140,000	Credit Cards	$20,000
Emergency Fund	$10,000	**Total Liabilities**	**$450,000**
Total Assets	**$1,950,000**	Net Worth = (Assets – Liabilities)	**$1,500,000**

Income Statement – Jones Family For Year Ending December 31, 20__	
Income	
Salary	$200,000
Investment Portfolio Income	$24,000
Total Income	**$224,000**
Expenses	
Home Mortgage	$30,000
Car Payments	$20,000
Credit Card Payments	$4,000
Living Expenses	$186,000
Total Expenses	**$240,000**
Net Income = (Income – Expenses)	-$16,000

The Smith Family

You'll notice the Smith family has a rental condo worth $500,000, with a corresponding mortgage of $200,000. Their total rental income is $2,000 per month, or $24,000 per year. Because their $15,000 condo mortgage payments and $5,000 expenses add up to $20,000 per year, they have positive cash flow of $4,000 per year from that investment ($24,000 – $20,000 = $4,000).

All the effort of managing a rental property may seem like a lot of work for $4,000 per year, but keep in mind that some-day the Smiths will pay the mortgage off. At that point, they'll have $24,000 of income with $5,000 in expenses, so the total positive cash flow will be more like $19,000 per year. That is probably a low estimate as inflation will likely cause rental income to increase faster than expenses over time.

The Smith family members are diligent savers, and their $700,000 investment portfolio provides $28,000 of income per year. We're assuming the portfolio contains a balanced mix of stocks and bonds, conservatively growing at 4% per year.

They have a mortgage of $410,000 on their $800,000 home, and the debt on their home goes down each month as they make their mortgage payments. At the same time, their home value is likely to increase over time at slightly higher than the rate of inflation.

The Case-Shiller US National Home Price Index, which measures repeat sales of house prices in the United States, rose from 100 in January 2000 to over 214 in January 2020. This indicates that home prices increased by just over 3.5% per year over that 20-year period. This is slightly higher than the 2.16% inflation rate over the same period, based on the Consumer Price Index for All Urban Consumers (CPI-U) reported by the Bureau of Labor Statistics.

The Smiths have no credit card debt or car loans. They saved up to pay cash for their two cars, a certified preowned Lexus sedan and SUV. They also maintain a cash emergency fund at their bank totaling $50,000, which would cover about three months of living expenses.

Notably, the Smith family's annual income is $32,000 greater than their yearly expenses. That means they have $32,000 that they can use to pay down debt or buy more income-producing assets.

Overall, the Smith family is in a solid financial position. They have a financial cushion if the unexpected happens, and they have made decisions that strengthen their balance sheet each month. Every month they receive rental income from their investment property and income from their investment portfolio. Because their income is higher than their expenses, they can channel that income into paying down their debt.

As they pay off their debt, their monthly expenses will go down. As their monthly expenses go down, their net income goes up. As their net income increases, they have a greater ability to pay down their debt. This will ideally continue until they are debt-free. They will eventually reach a stage where the income from their investments will be sufficient to maintain their lifestyle, at which point work becomes optional.

The Jones Family

Now let's look at the Jones family's financial situation. They have the same $200,000 annual salary as the Smith family, along with the same $1.5 million net worth. They also own a much more expensive home and cars than the Smiths do, so they look pretty wealthy on the surface.

However, things are not always what they seem. Even though the Jones family has less overall debt than the Smith family, almost a quarter of their debt comprises high-interest-rate credit card debt and car loans. Only the mortgage interest part of their debt is tax-deductible, while the Smith family can deduct all of their interest on their tax returns (as it is all related to mortgage interest).

Even though the Smiths have $610,000 of debt compared with the Joneses' $450,000 of debt, the Smiths pay less to service their debt due to this tax deductibility and the fact that they have no high-interest-rate credit card debt or car loans.

There is another glaring issue in the Joneses' income statement. Their total income is $224,000 per year, but their total expenses are $240,000 per year. That means that they are $16,000 in the hole this year, and they are digging themselves in deeper every year.

Their $20,000 credit card debt is growing because they have used their cards to make ends meet. They are paying $4,000 per year in interest due to the 20% interest rate, but that is not paying down any of the loan principal, so they are just treading water. That's $4,000 per year that they would otherwise be able to use to pay down debt, invest in income-producing assets, or just meet their living expenses.

They also only have $10,000 in their emergency fund, which is not enough to cover even one month's worth of living expenses.

The Joneses' income statement looks as bad as it does due to their spending decisions and habits. Unlike the Smiths, who bought preowned Lexus vehicles, the Joneses bought a brand-new Mercedes and BMW, both of which cost over $100,000 when new. They also purchased a much larger house than the Smiths, not realizing that the home's purchase price wasn't going to be the only expense. They didn't understand that everything costs more in the larger house, every month, for the entire time they own it.

The Smiths bought a 3,000-square-foot home, while the Joneses bought a house that is 50% larger, at 4,500 square feet. They didn't realize many things are approximately 50% more expensive to maintain or replace. For example, their cleaning service takes 50% longer, so they pay 50% more. That's $450 instead of $300 every month. When they replaced their carpets, both families paid $8 per square foot. It cost the Smiths $24,000, while it cost the Joneses $36,000. Property tax is

$8,000 per year for the Smiths and $12,000 per year for the Jones family.

These are just a few examples, but the total cost of ownership over time is significantly more expensive with the larger home. Having said that, it is true that if both homes go up in value by 10%, the Jones family's home will increase by $120,000, while the Smith family's home will increase by $80,000. But a home you live in should not be viewed primarily as an investment, as we'll discuss in the next section.

Borrowing money resulted in the Joneses' higher expenses, due to the higher interest rates on their debt. Their higher expenses meant they had no surplus income, making it harder for them to invest in assets. As they could not invest more in income-producing assets, they needed to borrow money to make ends meet. This vicious cycle of borrowing money, leading to higher expenses, followed by the need to borrow even more money, has been a slow, painful descent into bankruptcy for many unfortunate families.

Contrary to the old saying, the Smiths *do not* want to try keeping up with the Joneses.

Your Home: Asset or Liability?

A huge misconception is that a home is an asset, but it really isn't.

In *Rich Dad, Poor Dad*, Robert Kiyosaki makes the counterintuitive point that not every asset listed on your balance sheet is actually an asset. Remember the definition of an asset above? Assets are things you own that ideally produce income and increase in value. Producing income essentially means putting money in your pocket. Based on this definition, owning your own home would not be an asset.

Yes, it will likely increase in value over time. And it's possible to eventually downsize your home in retirement, using the equity to pay cash for a smaller home, which would allow you to invest the difference in income-producing assets.

Just remember that when you buy a home, you are paying for the mortgage, property taxes, maintenance, etc., and these expenses will offset the price appreciation the home experiences over time. Not to mention that if the home goes down in value during the period you own it, you have the double whammy of higher expenses and a more extensive loss if you need to sell at the lower price.

Still, homeownership has many advantages. It offers the opportunity to build equity over time, take advantage of tax deductions, and create a sense of security for your family. The size of your home is also a reflection of your values, so I'm not saying in any way that wanting a larger home is an unhealthy ambition.

Just don't confuse a home for an asset that's putting money into your pocket every month. Like the Smith family, if you buy a home you can afford and have surplus income above and beyond your expenses, you can purchase income-producing assets that do put money into your pocket each month.

In contrasting the Smith family with the Jones family, I was reminded of something that Zig Ziglar wrote in his book, *Born to Win*:

> When we make poor choices, our circumstances become worse. As our circumstances become worse, our choices become more limited. As our choices become more limited, the likelihood of making more bad choices is inevitable.
>
> On the other hand, when we make good choices, our circumstances improve. As our circumstances improve, we have better opportunities, and better opportunities make it possible for everything in our lives to become better. Once we begin to make certain types of choices, the likelihood of making similar choices in the future almost becomes a self-fulfilling destiny.

Ziglar's quote is a perfect description of the financial choices our hypothetical families made. The Jones family overspent and dug themselves into a hole. This further limited their choices and increased the likelihood of more bad choices, like creating more credit card debt.

In contrast, the Smith family developed good financial habits that improved their circumstances, giving them better opportunities. Those better opportunities further improved their situation, resulting in a virtuous cycle.

Put into financial terms, the Smith family developed good

financial habits that improved their net cash flow, giving them better opportunities, like the ability to invest in quality income-producing assets. Buying the income-producing assets further improved their circumstances by allowing them to pay off debt. Paying off their debt increased their net cash flow even more, which allowed them to invest in additional income-producing assets. In short, the Jones family spiraled down while the Smiths were spiraling up.

The Smiths' Upward Spiral

Let's look at how the Smith family created this virtuous cycle in a little more detail. Their first step was to make sure that their income was greater than their expenses. They did this in two ways. First, by investing in their education and developing skills, they increased their income. Second, by having the discipline to track their expenses and buy only what was necessary, they kept their expenses low. They also kept their debt low because higher debt leads to higher expenses. For example, a $30,000 car loan at 5% interest would have a payment of $566 per month. A $40,000 car loan with the same terms would have a payment of $755 per month. They understood that every additional dollar used to service their debt is one less dollar of net cash flow.

After generating positive net cash flow, they productively channeled those funds into their investment portfolio and their condo rental property. When those investments grew in value, their income surplus increased further, allowing them to pay down their debt, which allowed this virtuous cycle to continue.

As you can see, making prudent investment choices was a big part of improving their personal financial statement, so we'll discuss investments in greater detail below.

Investing Guidelines

Efficiency expert and business theorist Harrington Emerson said, "As to methods there may be a million and then some, but principles are few. The man who grasps principles can successfully select his own methods. The man who tries methods, ignoring principles, is sure to have trouble."

There are countless methods or approaches to investing, but following time-tested investing principles or guidelines will enable you to select the right approach for you. A list of proven investing guidelines is below. You may notice there is some overlap between the seven principles of financial serenity and our investing guidelines:

1. Have a plan to manage investment risk systematically

If your goal is to earn more than you can in a bank savings account, you will, by definition, need to take risks. Taking risks isn't necessarily bad, as long as you manage them by having a financial cushion should things not go your way and always have an exit strategy.

2. Keep your investment strategy simple

It's incredible how Wall Street and insurance companies continue to create esoteric investment products that even most financial advisors don't understand. The billionaire Warren Buffet once said, "Never invest in a business you cannot understand." I would take that one step further and say, "Never invest in *anything* you cannot understand."

3. Invest in low-cost, transparent, and liquid investment vehicles

One of the most accurate predictors of better investment performance is low fees, both in mutual funds and exchange-traded funds. That may sound like common sense since the lower the fees, the more you keep, but Morningstar and other research firms have run numerous studies to prove it. The same is true whether you're investing in commodities, bonds, or real estate.

Low fees go hand in hand with transparency, meaning you should be able to see what fees you're paying. And finally, it's recommended to invest in liquid investment vehicles, which means you can get your money out if you need it. Lack of liquidity is one of the drawbacks of investing in real estate. Investing in something like a condo rental property may make sense, but only if you have other investments that would allow you to access cash during an economic downturn.

4. Invest for total return, not just yield

When choosing an investment, some investors just care about price appreciation—for example, when a stock goes up from $50 per share to $60 per share. Other investors may just focus on yield, like buying a bond that pays 4% interest. A $1,000 bond that pays 4% interest would pay the investor a yield of $40 per year.

Total return accounts for both of these categories: income from dividends, distributions, or interest, and capital appreciation, which indicates an increase in the market price of an asset.

5. Do not mix entertainment and investing

I discussed this in Principle One: Focus On What You Can Control. Remember that investment programs on cable news channels exist to sell advertising, and they can charge more for their ad spots when they have more viewers. Sensational stories are entertaining and great for their bottom line, but they're detrimental to your equanimity and investment performance.

6. Do not allow tax considerations to drive investment decisions

Investments should be bought or sold based on their investment merits, not solely based on tax considerations. I've seen many investors buy an investment and not want to sell because they don't want to pay the taxes. In some cases, they ride it down and watch the investment gains disappear.

If you bought a stock at $100 per share that went to $200 per share, wouldn't it be better to sell and pay $20 of tax after pocketing an $80 gain rather than ride the investment back down to $100 and avoid paying the taxes?

7. Beware conflicts of interest

Very few people understand how financial advisors are compensated. Most are surprised when they learn the vast majority of financial advisors are paid through commissions or various kickbacks they receive for selling you products.

If an advisor gets a higher commission for selling you Product A than Product B, there's a good chance you're going to end up with Product A, whether it's the best investment for you or not. In contrast, clients pay fee-only financial advisors for the advice they give and the services they render.

The National Association of Personal Financial Advisors (NAPFA) defines a fee-only financial advisor as "one who is compensated solely by the client with neither the advisor nor any related party receiving compensation that is contingent on the purchase or sale of a financial product."

When the client pays the advisor directly for their advice, the advisor works for the client, not an insurance company or brokerage firm trying to maximize their own profits. By investing only with fee-*only* advisors, you know commissions do not cloud their investment recommendations with conflicts of interest. In contrast, fee-*based* advisors charge both fees and commissions.

As Kent Smetters, Wharton finance professor and host of SiriusXM Radio's *Your Money* program, says, "Only fee-only." He also says, "Don't be fooled by the expression 'fee-based'—that's a wolf in a sheep's clothing."

8. Remember that investing is a marathon, not a sprint

The value of every investment is going to fluctuate over time. On any given day, the stock market has about a 54% likelihood of going up and a 46% chance of going down. That means if you look at the market every single day, you're going to be disappointed almost half the time.

If you were to look at the change only at the end of each month, the market would be down about 33% of the time. If you were to look at the end of each year, it would only be down about 26% of the time. However, the stock market would only be down about 12% of the time if you look at returns over 10-year periods, and US markets have never lost money in 20-year periods.

In other words, by increasing the time horizon over which you evaluate your investment performance, you increase the chances that your investments will be up and that you'll follow your plan. Focusing on short-term gains and losses makes it more likely that you could panic and sell at the wrong time— not to mention the stress it can add to your life.

Every investor is different, and the assets you decide to invest in can vary greatly. The key is to develop a portfolio, or grouping of various financial assets, tailored to your goals and comfort with risk.

Looking beyond Investments

Income-producing assets are not the only way to improve the income side of your personal income statement. There's a limitless number of ideas out there, including starting a blog, affiliate marketing, renting out your home with Airbnb when you're away on vacation, selling products online, or starting a side business like pet sitting.

There are also limitless ideas for saving money to improve the expense side of your personal income statement. These ideas range from refinancing your home or car loan, consolidating debt to reduce your interest rate, installing LED lights in your home, canceling monthly memberships and subscriptions that you're not actively using, and buying nonperishable items in bulk.

The options to increase income and reduce expenses will change over time, but a quick online search will pop up hundreds of ideas to get you thinking.

What's most important is understanding these financial levers and believing you can improve your income statement over time. Armed with that knowledge, you can channel net cash flow into income-producing assets and paying down debt. Lower debt expense improves your income statement, leading to higher net worth, and the self-reinforcing, virtuous cycle will continue (more on the reasons to pay down debt in the next chapter).

John and Patricia:
Spiraling Up like the Smiths

John and Patricia are clients who retired in their early 60s. John was a midlevel manager at a manufacturing firm, and Patricia was a special education teacher. Their solid, stable incomes amounted to about double the US median household income. While that may sound like a lot, there was never a lot left over at the end of each month due to living in the high-cost area of Orange County, California.

However, they did have some advantages. They learned to distinguish an asset from a liability early on, and they committed to increasing the former and eliminating the latter. They decided early in their marriage that they would spend less than they earned and invest the difference.

They lived frugally and paid off their 30-year home mortgage after 24 years. They paid themselves first by investing 15% of every paycheck into a well-diversified portfolio of stocks and bonds. They weren't interested in investing in real estate since their home was worth significantly more than their stock and bond portfolio throughout most of their careers. They felt they'd be taking too much risk if they invested in real estate because their home and real estate investments could all plummet at once in a downturn.

Still, they didn't view the equity in their home as a retirement asset. They recognized that if they ever decided to downsize after their son and daughter moved out of their home, they would be able to use the leftover equity to buy income-producing assets.

For example, if they sold their $1 million home and downsized to a $600,000 low-maintenance, single-story property, they would be able to invest the $400,000 difference after accounting for transaction costs and taxes.

Throughout their careers, they simply viewed their home as a place in which to live. They understood the difference between assets, liabilities, income, and expenses, and they established good financial habits.

They made sure they had life insurance in the unlikely event one of them died when their kids were still minors. For the same reasons, they set up an estate plan, which also outlined their wishes if one or both of them became incapacitated. They always kept an emergency fund to cover six months of their spending needs.

They set up systems that allowed them to make small gains each month by automating their savings and having 15% of each paycheck go directly into their retirement accounts. Setting this up also offered the benefit of deferring taxes on their savings. As they paid their mortgage each month, their debt went down, and their net worth consequently went up.

Even though their income was never extraordinary, they saved a critical mass in their portfolio that today provides significant income for their retirement. Patricia also has a government pension equal to about 60% of her previous teaching income, and they combine that with their investment portfolio income.

They can now fly first class when they go on vacation, something they never did when they were focusing on improving their cash flow statement and balance sheet. By plowing their surplus income into their investments when they were younger, their investments now provide income for them to do what they want at this stage in their lives.

Will and Donna:
Spiraling Down like the Joneses

On the opposite end of the spectrum were Will and Donna, former clients in their early 50s and working toward retirement the last time we met. In retrospect, it wasn't a good match—they didn't like taking our advice, and we eventually went our separate ways.

Will was a skilled surgeon who earned about eight times the US median household income (about four times John and Patricia's income). Donna was a full-time mom dedicated to raising their kids.

Their household income put them in the highest federal and California tax brackets, which meant about half of their income went to taxes before they could spend or invest a dime.

Unfortunately, they spent money as if nothing had to be set aside for taxes. They bought a multimillion-dollar home, a $130,000 car, etc. These purchases increased their debt and reduced their assets, which in turn increased their expenses and reduced their net income.

Even though the doctor had saved hundreds of thousands of dollars into his pension plan, this vicious cycle eventually took its toll.

Their lack of savings was a constant source of conflict once we showed them how living beyond their means now would result in a spartan retirement unless they made some changes. In the end, they found another advisor whom they felt was a better fit.

Summary of Key Points

- Understanding your personal financial statement is vital to increasing your financial literacy and accelerating your financial success.
- Your personal financial statement consists of your personal balance sheet and your personal income statement.
- Your personal balance sheet summarizes what you own (assets) along with what you owe (liabilities). These two figures determine your net worth, which is simply your assets minus your liabilities.
- A personal income statement is a document that allows you to keep track of your monthly income sources and expenses at a glance. It primarily determines your net income over a certain period, like a month or a year. This is the result of subtracting your expenses from your income during that period.
- Income, expenses, assets, and liabilities are the four financial levers that control virtually everything in your financial life.
- Minimizing your expenses and increasing your income both result in increased net income. You can then channel that additional cash flow toward paying down debt or buying income-producing assets. Both of these

actions increase your net worth and further increase
your net income, resulting in a virtuous cycle of
spiraling up.

The Key Lesson

These stories demonstrate that it's less important *how much* money
you make, within obvious limits, and more important *what you
do* with your income. By understanding the financial levers in
your personal balance sheet and setting up systems to create
small wins over time, you can create a financial future that looks
more like John and Patricia's and less like Will and Donna's.

We Can Learn from Others' Mistakes and Successes

It's unfortunate Johnny Depp didn't understand what John and
Patricia did, but fortunately, you now do. Remember that debt
is a crucial part of your personal financial statement, and using
it wisely and paying it off is one of the seven principles of financial serenity, and that is what we'll cover in the next chapter.

Chapter 8

Principle Five:
Use Debt Wisely, and
Pay It Off

*"Think what you do when you run in debt; you give
to another power over your liberty."*

—**Benjamin Franklin**

*"Youth, never having had experience,
cannot realize that hopeless debt is like a deep pit
into which one may descend quickly and where
one may struggle vainly for many days."*

—**George S. Clason**, *The Richest Man in Babylon*

"It is the debtor that is ruined
by hard times."

—Former US President **Rutherford B. Hayes**

The Perils of Debt

Gallup ranked Michelle Obama as the most admired woman globally for the third year running in 2020. She is known for being a role model with grace, optimism, and humor. She's also known for her intelligence and work ethic, having graduated from Princeton and then Harvard Law School.

However, even she struggled with debt for much of her adult life. Despite embarking on a lucrative career in law, education, and healthcare after graduating from Harvard, she wasn't able to pay off her student loan debt until age 41, according to White House archives.

If you've struggled with debt, you're certainly not alone. While many people find themselves dealing with debt, few understand how detrimental it actually can be. Debt is dangerous because the amount you borrow can increase due to compound interest. Compound interest means that interest on the debt gets added to the amount you borrowed, and then the interest rate is applied to that larger balance. This can result in paying back significantly more than was initially borrowed, and more than you originally intended, to be free of the debt.

This never seems to come up in those credit card commercials you've seen for decades in which consumers are living large and well beyond their means, thanks to their friendly credit card company.

While the perils and advantages of debt might be a suitable topic for an extensive doctoral thesis, when it comes to personal finance, the short take is this: if you're going to use debt, use it wisely then pay it off. We'll unpack what "wisely" actually means, but it is not what the big banks have brainwashed us to believe.

Compound Interest: Working For or Against You?

Compound interest can be your worst enemy or your best friend, depending on whether you borrow money or invest it. Benjamin Franklin gave us a remarkable example of the power of compound interest over 200 years ago. In *The Elements of Investing: Easy Lessons for Every Investor* by Burton G. Malkiel and Charles D. Ellis, the authors recount the story:

> When Franklin died in 1790, he left a gift of $5,000 to each of his two favorite cities, Boston and Philadelphia. He stipulated that the money was to be invested and could be paid out at two specific dates, the first 100 years and the second 200 years after the date of the gift. After 100 years, each city was allowed to withdraw $500,000 for public works projects. After 200 years, in 1991, they received the balance—which

had compounded to approximately $20 million for each city. Franklin's example teaches all of us, in a dramatic way, the power of compounding. As Franklin himself liked to describe the benefits of compounding, "Money makes money. And the money that money makes, makes money."

The opposite is true when you borrow money and go into debt. Borrowed money costs money. And the money that costs money, costs money. That's why compound interest can either be wonderful or dangerous.

If your finances were a sailboat, interest earned would constantly fill your sails like a steady following wind and move you in the direction you want to go, but the interest paid would be a constant headwind.

In either case, the long-term effects can be staggering. Most people have no idea how powerful compound interest is, so we'll illustrate its potency using dollars in an example below.

Let's first consider how interest rates have changed over time. According to Federal Reserve Economic Data, the 30-Year Fixed Rate Mortgage in the United States has averaged just over 8% since 1971, although it has varied widely.

At an 8% interest rate, someone borrowing $500,000 to buy a home, and paying back that $500,000 over the following 30 years, would pay a whopping $820,000 in interest payments over that time frame. That's in addition to the original $500,000 of principal, which means they're paying $1.32 million to buy a home worth $500,000!

Now let's take a look at the other side of the balance sheet. If someone borrows $500,000 to buy a home at 8% interest over 30 years, it follows that a bank or investor is lending the homebuyer $500,000 and earning an interest rate of 8% per year. That investor is earning $820,000 in interest payments over that 30-year time frame, and they get their $500,000 back as well. That means they receive $1.32 million in total payments after lending the initial $500,000!

Albert Einstein put it succinctly when he reputedly said, "Compound interest is the eighth wonder of the world. He who understands it, earns it. He who doesn't, pays it."

What about My Home Mortgage?

As discussed in the previous chapter, buying a home may end up being a good long-term financial decision. Still, those aiming to spiral up financially should not borrow to buy more home than they need.

While a more expensive home could have a bigger increase in value than a less expensive home over time, remember that the more expensive home has proportionally higher expenses for all those years. That's why borrowing to buy a larger home than necessary can be a financial drain.

However, borrowing may be an excellent long-term decision in some situations. For example, borrowing could allow you to buy an investment condo, where the tenants' rental payments cover most or all of the mortgage.

Suppose your mortgage payments are fixed, and the rental income increases with inflation over the years. In that case, there will eventually be a surplus of income over your expenses, resulting in positive cash flow. Rental units also typically increase in value over time, which means you'll have a greater total return based on the surplus income and investment appreciation.

Are Student Loans Okay?

Borrowing can also be a great decision when investing in yourself, like when it's for education that improves your income. In 2021, EducationData.org reported the average cost for a public four-year institution paying out-of-state tuition is $174,884. That's an enormous investment, but consider that according to the Bureau of Labor Statistics (BLS), median weekly earnings for those with a bachelor's degree is $1,248 versus $746 for someone with a high school diploma and no college. That's an increase of $502 per week, or $26,104 per year. Using simple math and assuming a 40-year career, that's $1,044,160 in additional earnings for the $174,884 investment.

The BLS also reports that earnings increase across the board with higher levels of education. The message is clear: even if you have to use debt, investing in yourself can have a very high rate of return.

While it can make sense to use debt to invest in income-producing assets or education that increases future earnings, going into debt to buy toys or otherwise unaffordable vacations does not. Debt is best viewed as a temporary compromise to help achieve longer-term goals. The secret is not going into debt to buy more than you need and paying off the debt as soon as practicable. Remember from the previous chapter that reducing debt also reduces expenses, which increases net income and allows you to invest in income-producing assets.

Simple Debt Repayment Strategies

Now that we know why we should reduce debt, let's explore methods to do so. First, make sure to pay at least the minimum every month on all of your loans. Missing a payment leads to a lower credit score, which means paying higher interest rates on future loans.

For credit card loans, it's advisable to pay more than the minimum if possible. Consistently paying only the minimum amount may be seen as a red flag that could cause a lower credit score, a reduced credit line, and a higher interest rate.

Making the minimum loan payment on time every month for cars, mortgages, and student loans will generally strengthen your credit score and save money over the long run.

Debt Avalanche Strategy

The next step is to use the debt avalanche strategy, listing all debts, with the highest interest rate loan at the top and the lower interest rate loans below that in descending order.

Once you have your list of loans, pay as much as you can afford toward the highest interest rate loan. After you totally pay off that loan, use the money you were paying toward that debt to pay down the next debt in line. Repeat this for each loan until you pay off all of the debt.

Let's look at an example using the table below:

Loan	Balance	Interest Rate	Payment
Visa Credit Card	$6,500	24%	$195
Target Credit Card	$1,700	22%	$51
Car Loan	$25,000	7%	$495
Mortgage	$300,000	5%	$1,610

In this example, we assume credit card minimum payments are 3% of the monthly balance. The car loan payment uses a five-year amortization schedule, and the mortgage payment uses a 30-year amortization schedule.

If you had the above loans, you would first make sure you're paying the minimum payment on all four loans. After looking at your monthly cash flow, you might determine you could put an extra $200 per month toward paying off debt. That means you would pay $395 instead of the $195 minimum payment toward your Visa credit card each month.

As soon as you pay off the Visa, you could start to apply that $395 toward your Target credit card, on top of the $51 minimum payment you've already been making. That means $446 would be going toward paying down the Target credit card each month.

As soon as you pay off that credit card, you will be able to put an additional $446 toward your car payment each month, for a total of $941. After you pay off the car loan, you will be able to put an additional $941 toward the mortgage.

The debt avalanche strategy outlined above is effective because it minimizes the amount of interest you pay.

Debt Snowball Strategy

Another strategy called the debt snowball ranks the loan balances from smallest to largest. Re-sorting the table above by loan balance would mean paying off the Target credit card first, followed by the Visa, the car loan, and finally the mortgage. This method gives a psychological boost from quick wins as you pay off each loan.

Using the debt snowball method, the table would look like this:

Loan	Balance	Interest Rate	Payment
Target Credit Card	$1,700	22%	$51
Visa Credit Card	$6,500	24%	$195
Car Loan	$25,000	7%	$495
Mortgage	$300,000	5%	$1,610

In this example, we assume credit card minimum payments are 3% of the monthly balance. The car loan payment uses a five-year amortization schedule, and the mortgage payment uses a 30-year amortization schedule.

Although I prefer the debt avalanche method because it minimizes the amount of interest you pay, I understand how the debt snowball approach could be the better overall choice for those energized by getting quick wins. This is true as long as the interest rate difference is not too substantial.

Only you can determine the best approach for yourself, but it is generally the one that will motivate you to pay down your debt as quickly as possible.

Debt Payoff Tactics

Another way to pay off debt is to make sure you're paying the lowest interest rate you can get. That starts with having excellent credit, so you get the best available interest rates on the loans you take out. The way to get stellar credit starts with paying your bills on time, every time.

It's also helpful to keep your credit utilization rate low, meaning you only borrow a small percentage of the credit available to you. As an example, if you have a credit limit of $20,000 on your various credit cards but only borrow $1,000, your credit utilization rate is a low 5% ($1,000 divided by $20,000).

Also, try to minimize your credit inquiries. Every time you apply for a new credit card, auto loan, or mortgage, the lender will issue a credit check, and too many inquiries may raise red flags by signaling overspending.

If you're a homeowner, keep an eye on interest rates and refinance when it makes sense. For example, if rates drop from 5% to 4% on the 30-year fixed mortgage loan above, the payment will drop from $1,610 per month to $1,432 per month, saving $2,136 per year.

Sid and Janice: Fixing a Debt Misstep

When Sid and Janice were in their late 50s, they decided to downsize their home in high-income-tax California and move to no-income-tax Nevada in preparation for retirement.

Sid traveled extensively in his role as a management consultant, and Janice's career as a flight attendant meant they could live virtually anywhere near an airport. They thought they could sell their California home for over $800,000, pay off their $300,000 mortgage, and buy a home in Nevada for around $500,000 cash. Having no mortgage would take a lot of pressure off their monthly expenses and allow them to make work optional. Unfortunately, things didn't work out as planned.

Before they sold their California home, they began looking at homes in Nevada. While many available homes were in the $500,000 range, none of them inspired them to move such a long way. They gradually started looking at homes in the $550,000 to $600,000 range. They finally found their dream home for $620,000, made an offer that was accepted, and couldn't wait to make the move.

They listed their California home for over $800,000 on the advice of their overly optimistic real estate agent. However, they had to cut the price three times before it sold for $730,000. After the realtor's 5% commission, they netted $694,000, which became $394,000 after paying off their $300,000 mortgage.

Instead of paying cash for their Nevada home as planned, they ended up buying a $620,000 home with $394,000 in cash and took out a $226,000 mortgage.

Their Nevada property taxes were only 0.90%, which was lower than the 1.2% rate they were paying in California. However, their California home was under Proposition 13. Prop 13 limited property tax increases to no more than 2% per year, as long as the property was not sold.

Therefore, even though Sid and Janice's California home was worth over $700,000, they only paid 1.2% of the assessed value, which was $400,000, for a total tax of $4,800 per year. The 0.90% tax rate on their new $620,000 Nevada home resulted in higher property taxes of $5,580 per year. While this additional cost is not that significant, it was an unexpected and hidden cost of moving.

The move itself cost about $10,000, and once they were settled, they realized they needed to renovate portions of the home to really make it their own. The renovations cost $70,000, and they paid for these two expenses with an $80,000 second mortgage.

Thus, their total debt on the new home was $306,000,

which meant a mortgage payment (principal and interest only) of a little over $1,500 per month.

Most of their investment assets were in their IRA accounts, so those funds had never been taxed. Whenever someone withdraws money from an IRA account, they must pay income taxes. Even though Nevada has no state income taxes, the 22% federal income tax meant that if they retired and decided to pay their mortgage from their IRA accounts, they would have to withdraw almost $2,000 every month to pay $1,500 toward their first and second mortgages.

Therefore, they would need to withdraw $2,000 from their investment accounts automatically every month, and that wouldn't cover paying for groceries or any other expenses. The biggest challenge was that the mortgage payments were scheduled to continue for the next 30 years. Fortunately, they were still both employed, so they could make their payments from their monthly employment income and didn't need to begin taking IRA withdrawals yet.

They realized too late that the move was a net drain on their finances. They loved their new home, though, and decided to put themselves in a stronger financial situation. They made paying off the $306,000 debt their number one priority.

After they completed the home renovations, they put a freeze on additional home improvement spending. Janice worked extra flights, resulting in more income and reduced expenses as she spent less money when away from home. Sid started a blog related to his management consulting work, which brought in some extra income through affiliate marketing.

It took seven years, but their combined incomes allowed them to pay off their debt in their mid-60s. Now, they are completely debt-free and have maintained their habit of keeping expenses low.

Paying off the first and second mortgage loans meant their income was no longer going toward housing. This reduced their expenses and increased their monthly net income, which allowed them to channel more of their income into their investment accounts.

Being debt-free also allowed them to maximize their Social Security benefits, which is a critical financial decision. After we evaluated their Social Security claiming strategy options, they decided to wait until they both turned age 70 to file for benefits.

Social Security recipients are eligible to claim benefits as early as age 62. However, claiming benefits early means they'll receive a reduced amount, and that lower amount will continue for the rest of their lives. This is rarely the optimal decision.

Those who wait until full retirement age (FRA) will receive their "full benefit" amount. FRA is based on your birth year but ranges from age 66 to 67. However, it's important to note that "full benefit" is lower than the maximum benefit. Waiting to claim benefits at age 70 will result in getting the maximum benefit.

In Sid and Janice's case, their Social Security benefits were as follows:

	Age 62 Monthly Benefit	Age 66 Monthly Benefit (FRA)	Age 70 Monthly Benefit
Sid	$2,265	$3,011	$3,790
Janice	$1,810	$2,390	$3,026

Using our financial planning software, we found that if they were to claim benefits when they both reached their full retirement age, they could expect to receive total lifetime benefits of $1.66 million, assuming at least one of them lives into their early 90s.

By delaying benefits until age 70, the higher monthly benefits would result in a total lifetime Social Security income of $1.82 million. This is a difference of about $160,000 of additional income.

There is a catch, however. If they knew they'd only live until age 68, for example, it would make sense to take Social Security as early as possible. In their case, the break-even age for delaying benefits until age 70 is age 79.

In other words, as long as they live beyond age 79, it would make sense for them to delay taking benefits until age 70 because that would give them time to more than make up for the lost monthly income between age 66 and age 70.

Even though they haven't taken Social Security yet, they are in a position where work is already optional. Their investments now generate income that, combined with Janice's airline pension, more than covers their monthly expenses. When they begin taking Social Security at age 70, they'll be in an even stronger financial position.

They're in such a strong position now largely because they are debt-free. When they had hundreds of thousands of dollars of debt costing them interest each month, they were limited in their ability to save, invest, and earn interest.

Now their investment accounts continue to grow, and they are benefitting from the assets on their balance sheet. Compound interest is filling their sails each month instead of acting as a headwind.

When to Use Debt

While debt is necessary for most people at some point in their lives, managing debt well is a key factor in spiraling up financially. Most of us need to take out a loan to buy our first car or our first home. Beyond that, we should only take out debt for two main reasons.

The first reason is to invest in assets that will likely pay off in the future, such as a rental property that provides positive cash flow. The second reason is to invest in ourselves. If we need to borrow for things such as earning a college degree, starting a business, or getting a certification that will allow us to earn more in the future, we can use assumptions and basic math to determine if it's a good idea or not.

There is no third reason to go into debt. Simply remember

that if you're going to use debt, use it wisely and then pay it off. This is one component of a well-thought-out plan that, combined with discipline, will allow you to achieve your financial goals and retire comfortably.

Summary of Key Points

- Compound interest is incredibly powerful. It can work for you when you make investments, but it can work against you when you borrow money.
- It can be beneficial to take on debt to invest in income-producing assets or education that increases future earnings. However, going into debt to buy consumer goods or take a vacation makes no sense.
- Debt is best viewed as a temporary compromise to help achieve longer-term goals, and it is helpful to pay it off as soon as practicable.
- An effective way to pay off debt is to use the debt avalanche strategy, in which you rank the loans by interest rate and pay off the highest interest rate loan first, followed by the others in order.
- Another method is the debt snowball strategy, where you rank the loan balances from smallest to largest. You pay off the smallest loan first, followed by the others in order.

- To minimize the cost of your debt, make sure you're paying the lowest interest rate possible. Do everything in your power to maximize your credit score, and refinance to a lower interest rate when possible.

Sticking with the Plan

We've seen that even though Michelle Obama went into debt for a good reason as it was an investment in her future earning ability, she still carried her student loan debt until age 41. It's okay to pay back debt slowly in some cases. The key is that we view debt as temporary and always stick with our plan to pay it off. One of the best ways to pay that debt off is to develop good financial habits, and we'll explore how to do that next in our discussion of the sixth principle of achieving financial serenity.

Chapter 9

Principle Six:
Develop Good Financial Habits

"And ultimately, people do not decide their future;
they decide their habits and their habits
decide their future."

—**John C. Maxwell**, *New York Times*
bestselling author and leadership expert

"Sow an action and you reap a habit;
sow a habit and you reap a character;
sow a character and you reap a destiny."

—**Anonymous**

"It doesn't matter how successful or unsuccessful
you are right now. What matters is whether your habits
are putting you on the path toward success. You should be far
more concerned with your current trajectory than with your
current results. If you're a millionaire but you spend more than
you earn each month, then you're on a bad trajectory;
if your spending habits don't change, it's not going to end well.
Conversely, if you're broke, but you save more than you
spend every month, then you're on the path toward
financial freedom . . ."

—**James Clear**, *New York Times*
bestselling author, *Atomic Habits*

"My actions are my only true belongings:
I cannot escape the consequences of my actions.
My actions are the ground on which I stand."

—**Thich Nhat Hanh**, internationally acclaimed
94-year-old Buddhist monk, peace activist,
and author, *The Heart of the Buddha's Teaching*

Good Habits Mean Better Results

In the previous chapter on paying off debt, we learned that
compound interest could be your best friend or your worst
enemy, depending on which side of the balance sheet you're

on. We heard the story of how Benjamin Franklin's $10,000 gift turned into over $40 million through the power of compound interest.

Recall that Franklin said, "Money makes money. And the money that money makes, makes money." The same is true with good habits. Good habits make progress. And the progress that good habits make, makes more progress.

Just as compound interest allows for the exponential growth of your money over time, good financial habits allow for exponential progress toward your financial goals.

Small Improvements, Big Results

Good financial habits are essential simply because they lay the foundation for financial security, independence, freedom, and serenity.

In *Atomic Habits*, James Clear writes:

Habits are the compound interest of self-improvement. The same way that money multiplies through compound interest, the effects of your habits multiply as you repeat them. They seem to make little difference on any given day and yet the impact they deliver over the months and years can be enormous. It is only when looking back two, five, or perhaps ten years later that the value of good habits and the cost of bad ones becomes strikingly apparent.

To visualize what he means, think about an account balance hypothetically compounding at 1% per day, versus losing 1% per day. You can see this in the chart below.

It shows the effect of $1,000 growing by 1% per day. As you can see, $1,000 increases to a whopping $37,409 after 365 days. On the other hand, if that same $1,000 were to lose 1% per day, the account balance would drop all the way down to $26 after 365 days.

While a 1% change doesn't seem like much from one day to the next, the difference between $26 and $37,409 is staggering.

**The Value of $1,000
Gaining or Losing 1% per Day**

Value of $1,000 compounding at 1% per day
Value of $1,000 losing 1% per day

The next big idea from *Atomic Habits* is that while goals can be useful, systems built by habits are more powerful than goals. The third big idea is that every action you take is a vote for the person you want to become, so each time you take even a small action, you're reinforcing your new identity.

Good Habits Make Even Better Habits Possible

Good habits build on each other—developing one makes it easier to develop others.

Five years ago, I read *The Life-Changing Magic of Tidying Up* by Marie Kondo. At first blush, the book appears to be about organizing your belongings, but it's really about prioritizing what you want in your life and eliminating the things that don't bring you joy.

The blogosphere is teeming with posts about how that book changed readers' lives for the better. Those who developed the sound tidying habits Kondo recommended talk about the many other positive yet seemingly unrelated results they experienced, including losing weight, making more money, and having better relationships, among many others.

Once you're clear on what brings you joy, certain habits change. You're less likely to overspend on things you'd end up throwing away after having them for a short time. Once your home is uncluttered, you'll think twice before buying something that's going to clutter it up. When everything is arranged in the way you want, it's much easier to keep everything in its place. Anything out of place stands out like a sore thumb, so keeping things neat becomes almost automatic.

I found that upgrading my home and office environments through her method positively affected the other areas of my life. This happened because each area of our lives is related to every other area. Whether it's your physical environment, finances, career, relationships, or your health, you experience negative or positive feelings at any given moment. Negative feelings in one area bring your energy down in the other areas, while positive feelings bring your energy up in the other areas.

For example, having a bad day at work can negatively affect your relationships with your spouse or kids that night. In contrast, positive energy in one area can lead to improvements in the other areas. Having a clean, well-organized physical environment in your home or office can improve your performance at work, which is another great example of spiraling up. This is why little habits are so important: the small things are the foundation for the big things in our lives.

We either form our habits or they develop by default, but regardless of how we get our habits, they then begin to form us. The good news is that we can choose to form the habits we want to achieve our desired outcomes.

How Do We Form Good Habits?

BJ Fogg is one of the world's leading authorities on the science of behavior change and the founder of the Behavior Design Lab at Stanford University. He is also the author of *Tiny Habits: The Small Changes That Change Everything*. One of his key insights is that, as the title of his book suggests, good habits are more likely to stick if you start by making small changes.

Because the theory behind behavior change is a more extended discussion, a detailed summary of Fogg's research, as applied to developing better financial habits, can be found in Appendix D: Keys to Developing Better Financial Habits. For now, it's just key to know that the idea of making big progress by starting small is backed by science proving the effectiveness of this approach.

What Are the Good Financial Habits That We Want to Create?

Just as there are seven principles to achieving financial serenity, there are seven financial habits we want to cultivate.

1. Prepare for the unexpected

Writer and math professor John Allen Paulos said, "Uncertainty is the only certainty there is, and knowing how to live with insecurity is the only security." That's why it's so important to make sure you have a plan for the unexpected, especially when it comes to your finances.

Protecting yourself and your family typically starts with insurance and estate planning, which can both address very unlikely but potentially disastrous events, such as an unexpected death, illness, or accident.

It's also crucial to have an emergency fund, cash you can quickly access in the event of an unanticipated expense, an illness, or the loss of your job. It's a good idea to keep a minimum of three to six months of living expenses on hand.

For example, someone who spends $5,000 per month would need between $15,000 and $30,000 in their emergency fund. Those with less stable sources of income, like entrepreneurs, may want to have more like 12 months of cash in their emergency fund.

Your stock market investments don't count toward the emergency fund because stocks are sometimes subject to wild swings. Somehow, it seems the market is usually down when these income or expense disruptions occur, and you don't want to be forced to sell good assets into a bad market.

(More on preparing for the unexpected in the next chapter.)

2. Save for goals within two years

If you're planning on buying a car, taking an extended vacation, or putting a down payment on a home in the next couple of years, it's helpful to get in the habit of saving for those things now. This will give you a sense of control over your finances and reduce your stress when you eventually spend the money. For example, studies show that going on vacation is more relaxing when it's paid for before the trip instead of afterward.

Just remember that these savings, like the savings in your emergency fund, should be held in a guaranteed FDIC-insured account. Investing these funds in stocks or bonds is not a good idea because you're risking that the price of those investments could drop right before you need to use the funds.

3. Pay yourself first

Paying yourself first means saving or investing the money you earn before paying monthly expenses or making discretionary purchases. Legendary investor Warren Buffett said, "Don't save what is left after spending; spend what is left after saving."

It's recommended to save at least 15% of everything you make. This may be difficult initially, but it becomes easier as the habit develops, especially as you get accustomed to the strangely good feeling that comes with watching your finances strengthen and grow.

My first job out of college was as a US Navy submarine officer in 1992, and I made about $2,000 per month. There was no way I could have saved 15% of my income at the outset because $300 was a lot of money when you only have $2,000 per month to cover all expenses.

However, I was able to save $150 per month initially, and I resolved to increase my savings as my earnings increased. When I advanced to the rank of lieutenant junior grade, I got a raise of $400 per month. At that point, I took half of my increase, $200, and added it to the $150 per month I was already saving, for a total of $350 per month. Now, I was saving just under 15% of my income ($350 divided by $2,400).

Each time I got a raise or promotion, I took half of the increase and added it to my monthly savings and investment amount. The beauty of this simple habit is that every time my income went up, I got to enjoy spending part of the increase, but I was also saving and investing more at the same time. The benefit of this method is that I didn't feel like I was sacrificing anything as I was never accustomed to spending my entire paycheck.

It was also much easier because I put this process on auto-pilot by setting up automatic transfers. The transfers automatically went into my savings and investment accounts as soon as my paycheck appeared in my checking account.

Automatic transfers are discussed in more detail in the Automate Your Finances section below.

4. Spend mindfully

Mindful spending means buying things in accordance with your values instead of buying things society tells you that you should value. Mindful spending can take many forms.

Sometimes it means supporting local small businesses instead of a large corporate chain. Sometimes it means not spending any money at all. Other times it means spending twice as much on an item you love and will leave as an heirloom to your grandchildren, instead of spending half as much on a similar item that will end up in a landfill after a few months.

The central idea is that you're checking in with your core values and spending money accordingly. Of course, spending based on your core values requires a good understanding of what those core values are. Again, you can see Appendix A: Values Worksheet if you'd like to explore your values in greater detail.

In addition to the emotional benefits from aligning your values and actions, mindful spending can also help us spend less. We're less likely to spend money on something we don't need if we're not trying to keep up with the Joneses.

Another strategy to spend less is to track your spending. You can do this using a program like Mint.com, a free online tool that allows you to review all of your accounts and financial transactions at a glance. Or, you can do it with pen and paper. By tracking all your spending for even one month, you gain awareness of areas where you may be overspending, making it easier to develop better spending habits.

Author David Bach immortalized the concept of the Latte Factor, which teaches that small amounts of money spent on things like lattes could be invested instead, leading to more robust savings and wealth. This is good to keep in mind.

Nonetheless, Catey Hill of *MarketWatch* asserts that the act of watching every single purchase you make has its limits. Constantly having to make choices on smaller items could result in decision fatigue, a phenomenon where our ability to make good choices worsens throughout the day.

Instead of constantly tracking small expenses, it may be more effective to be mindful of your largest expenses. Hill cites TD Ameritrade research identifying a group of Americans whose savings rate topped 20% and dubbing them "Super Savers." One of the most eye-catching statistics in their study is that Super Savers spend only 14% of their income on housing, while the average American spends 23%. They also only spend 8% on cars, instead of 11% for the average American.

Housing and cars are two of the largest parts of most Americans' budgets, so spending mindfully here is a great way to maximize savings. We only decide to make these purchases once every several years, and saving 15% on housing will save a lot more money than saving 15% on smaller items.

As the ideas in this book begin to coalesce in your mind, you may decide to switch from spending most of your discretionary income to saving and investing some of that money instead.

As a thought experiment, consider all the hard-earned dollars you spend with retailers, on fashion, and for weekend getaways. This helps companies like Amazon, Ralph Lauren, and Hilton, transferring part of your wealth to those major corporations at the expense of your savings and investment goals.

That spending helps make those corporations grow, become wealthy, and expand.

What would happen if, instead, you reduced that discretionary outflow and diverted it into a retirement account that invests in the stock of these corporations? You would switch from contributing to *their* growth, wealth, and success to directly participating in that growth, wealth, and success yourself—funded by the other 90% of consumers who do not embrace mindful spending.

This is not to suggest that discretionary spending needs to stop. It simply provides an opportunity if you decide to *reduce* your discretionary spending. Seen in this light, you can contribute less to major consumer corporations' growing wealth and instead invest and participate in it yourself.

In her book *The Year of Less*, author Cait Flanders decided to stop shopping for an entire year, only buying necessities like groceries and consumables. She had already paid off her almost $30,000 of consumer debt, but when her bad consumer habits started to take hold again, she decided on the one-year shopping ban.

When her one-year experiment was over, she said:

> I gave up the things marketers try to convince us we should want in life: the newest and greatest of everything, anything that can fix our problems, and whatever is in style. I exchanged it all for basic necessities, and after a year of not being able to buy anything new, realized that was all I needed. That was

all anybody needed. I had always been stuck in the cycle of wanting more, buying more, and then needing more money. The ban uncovered the truth, which was that when you decide to want less, you can buy less and ultimately need less money.

Her income that year was $55,000, and she was able to live on $28,000 while saving $17,000 and spending the remaining $10,000 on travel. She realized through the shopping ban that she had never actually valued all of the pricey consumer goods she had purchased. By banning that type of shopping, she had more time and money to travel and visit with friends and family, which aligned her spending with her values. Fortunately, we can learn from her experience and align our own spending with our own values.

5. Pay down debt

In addition to being a principle that leads to financial serenity, paying down debt is also a habit.

Some people get in the habit of bringing on more and more debt because they think they'll win the lottery, their income will increase, the universe will provide, or tomorrow will never come. This is not a good strategy.

By getting in the habit of paying down debt, especially high-interest-rate credit card debt, you're minimizing your expenses and taking control of your financial future.

Additionally, other than when it comes to that first car or house, if you maintain the discipline of paying off debt and not borrowing money for future purchases, you will come face to face with the practicality of each and every purchase.

If you must write a check for the entire amount for your next car, vacation, or latest tech gadget, the full reality of that expense is not a vague notion to be dealt with later just because you can handle the monthly payments. While those things provide a quick mood boost initially, that rarely equals the feeling of watching your finances grow and realizing your goals.

An Ancient Stoic Exercise in Resilience (and Mindful Spending)

Seneca was a Roman Stoic philosopher, writer, and statesman in the first century AD. He had the unenviable position of serving as an advisor to the tyrannical and cruel Emperor Nero. Because Seneca lived during a time of great uncertainty, he was always looking for ways to immunize himself from the shifting winds of fortune.

In *Moral Letters to Lucilius*, he advised his friend to:

Set aside a certain number of days, during which you shall be content with the scantiest and cheapest fare, with coarse and rough dress, saying to yourself the while: "Is this the condition that I feared?" It is precisely in times of immunity from care that the soul should toughen itself beforehand for occasions of greater stress, and it is while Fortune is kind that it should fortify itself against her violence...

Seneca was advising his friend to set aside time without his normal luxuries so he could see that life without those things isn't as bad as he was subconsciously making it out to be. By deliberately practicing this type of discomfort, any unexpected hardships would have less of an effect. Some have taken this advice to extremes and regularly fast for several days or sleep on the hard floor instead of in their beds.

However, we can benefit from this type of exercise without going to any extremes. For example, we can set aside a weekend where we decide not to spend any money at all. We can eat only the food we have in the kitchen and enjoy all types of free entertainment. With a bit of imagination, there are countless free activities we can experience.

Maybe going for a walk in nature, feeding ducks at a local pond, or just people-watching at a mall without spending any money would be something you'd enjoy. Then you could pack a simple picnic lunch with whatever you have on hand in the kitchen (cheese and crackers, cold cuts, and those green olives you have in the back of the fridge) and watch the sunset. It's amazing how good simple food can taste if you slow down and appreciate it.

This exercise reminds us that some of the greatest pleasures in life cost little or nothing. Realizing we can enjoy so many things without spending any money also gives us the confidence to take risks we may not otherwise take, like starting a business or taking a job that pays less but is more fulfilling.

As billionaire investor Ray Dalio writes in his book, *Principles*:

Having the Basics—a good bed to sleep in, good relationships, good food, and good sex—is most important, and those things don't get much better when you have a lot of money or much worse when you have less.

6. Automate your finances

In the introduction to this chapter, I said good habits make progress. And the progress that good habits make, makes more progress. Automating your finances is a case in point.

Automating your finances by setting up automatic bill pay for all of your monthly expenses will result in having more time and less stress. This could free you up to build on that progress in other areas, perhaps by setting up automatic transfers into your savings and investment accounts.

After everything is automated, you'll have even more additional time and even fewer distractions, like having to remember to pay bills. This will give you the mental clarity to focus on other areas that will improve your life, financial or otherwise.

Automating your bill paying and savings is a great start. Then, you can set up automatic investments to a health savings account (HSA) if eligible. HSAs allow for a tax deduction when contributing money to the account. The money grows tax-free and can be withdrawn tax-free, as long as it is used for medical expenses. It's one of the most favorable areas of the tax code.

Next, you can set up automatic contributions to your 401(k), if applicable, up to the employer match. If you're able to save beyond that level, you can increase your contributions accordingly. If you don't have a company 401(k) but earn income from your job, you can contribute to a traditional IRA or Roth IRA account to save on a tax-advantaged basis.

Finally, if you want to reduce taxes while saving for college, whether it's for yourself, a child, or a grandchild, you can open and set up automatic contributions to a 529 college savings plan.

7. Take action

The final habit we want to cultivate is taking action. Because finances can be intimidating, it's easy to fall into the trap of analysis paralysis. However, doing nothing can cost you when it comes to your finances.

For example, a client left $240,000 sitting in a bank savings account at 0.05% interest. At that rate, he was getting paid $120 per year in annual interest. We showed him that an FDIC-insured online bank was paying 1.75% interest at the time. He moved his money to the online bank, which paid him $4,200 in annual interest. An additional $4,080 in annual income wasn't bad for around 30 minutes of work!

Former president Theodore Roosevelt said, "In any moment of decision, the best thing you can do is the right thing, the next best thing is the wrong thing, and the worst thing you can do is nothing." When it comes to your finances, get into the habit of taking action. If your initial action happens to be wrong, you can make course corrections by taking further action.

We had another client who had a $500,000, 30-year home mortgage fixed at a rate of 5%. With interest rates near generational lows in 2021, mortgage rates also came down significantly. She thought refinancing might be a good idea, but she heard that higher lending standards made it difficult to qualify for a mortgage refinance.

When we met for our annual review, she expressed her doubts about qualifying for a new loan because she was retired and couldn't show income from a paycheck. It was clear she was fearful of getting rejected by the lender.

We asked if we could refer her to an outstanding independent mortgage broker we know. We told her the worst thing that could happen is the banks could say no, but we thought she had a decent chance of qualifying for the refinance, and she agreed.

Our mortgage broker colleague got her a new loan at 3.25%, saving her over $6,000 per year on her loan payments and consequently improving her cash flow. Taking action helped her get over her doubts and put her in a stronger financial position.

As Dale Carnegie said, "Inaction breeds doubt and fear. Action breeds confidence and courage. If you want to conquer fear, do not sit home and think about it. Go out and get busy."

Michael and Debra: A Comfortable Retirement Built through Habits

Michael and Debra came to us eight years ago, when he was 56 and she was 54. They had never developed a financial plan before they met us, mainly due to inertia. They didn't see a pressing need to create a plan because they were doing well financially overall.

In fact, they didn't think much about their financial future at all until a year before they met us, when Michael's 81-year-old mom came to them asking for money to help with her monthly bills. This was a huge wake-up call for them. Even though they could afford to help Michael's mom, they wanted to make sure they didn't end up in her situation someday, and that's what spurred them to contact us.

We learned about their entire financial situation during our initial meeting and gained insights into their formative experiences with money.

Debra's parents owned a wholesale plumbing supply

business, and she remembered her dad's habit of meticulously tracking inventory, expenses, income, and the family's wealth. His favorite expression was, "You get what you measure," and he explained that tracking those things helped the family reach their goals over time.

Her parents also taught her some keen financial insights. Debra remembers them telling her and her two siblings that even though some of their neighbors had boats and nicer cars, that didn't necessarily mean they were rich as they could have bought those things by going heavily into debt.

Michael grew up in a solidly middle-class family where their income covered their needs and most of their wants. They could afford to eat out in restaurants every Friday and take a weeklong vacation every summer and winter.

However, his parents divorced when he was in high school, and the family's finances took a turn for the worse. Michael watched as both parents struggled to make ends meet because all of a sudden, they were maintaining two households on essentially the same income. Watching how everything unfolded, he realized that some of his parents' financial challenges would have been less severe had they saved for a rainy day during the years they were married.

Michael said that over time, his dad began to do everything he could to repair his finances. He read avidly and made some wise investments over the years. About 10 years after Debra and Michael got married, his dad gave them his tattered copy of one of his favorite books, *The Millionaire Next Door*.

That was in 2000, a few years after the book was initially published, and it reinforced some of their early financial lessons. Despite some of these essential lessons, Debra and Michael admitted to making financial mistakes early in their marriage, such as racking up credit card debt for vacations and unexpected expenses.

After reading the book, they resolved to develop more positive financial habits and make a clear distinction between their needs and wants.

When we created their initial financial plan, it was the first time they saw all of their assets, liabilities, income, and expenses in one document. Seeing how we calculated their net worth was eye-opening. Subtracting their debts right off the top of their assets gave them a whole new perspective. More specifically, their $1 million home didn't look nearly as impressive when shown next to their $350,000 mortgage. This made them realize the importance of paying off their debts.

They decided to make a habit of tracking expenses using Mint.com and put their surplus income toward paying down their mortgage. Once they started paying down their debt aggressively, they began to find contentment and even joy in saving, not spending, which further reinforced the habit.

Using Mint.com also helped them keep tabs on their expenses after they gave their teenage daughters credit cards. Debra would check the card activity at least twice per week. This simple habit allowed them to deal with potential problems like getting close to card limits before they became an issue.

These small wins inspired them to focus on other helpful financial habits. They learned to prepare for the unexpected, save for goals within two years, pay themselves first, and spend mindfully. They also automated their finances where possible and made a habit of taking action whenever they saw a way to put themselves in a stronger financial position.

Once their daughters were in their late teenage years, Debra and Michael were in good enough financial shape to retire. Even though Debra didn't necessarily have to work outside the home any longer, she decided to work part-time because her job as a speech therapist gave her that flexibility.

Then as they neared retirement, Debra reduced her hours even further. They prepared for retirement by living off Michael's income only for one year, and they put all of Debra's income in savings.

That gave them the confidence to take the next big step, which was for them both to retire. They retired last year and are currently living off their investments and Michael's small pension. They decided to delay taking Social Security until they're in their late 60s to allow their benefits to grow. When they begin taking Social Security in a few years, they'll be able to reduce the income they withdraw from their investment accounts.

Michael and Debra are thrilled to be retired with the time and financial resources to travel. They both credit their willingness to seek out a financial planner and develop the right financial habits for getting them in the comfortable position they're in now.

Summary of Key Points

- Good financial habits allow you to realize exponential progress when it comes to achieving your financial goals.
- It's easy to underestimate the long-term effects of small changes. As an analogy, starting with a $1,000 investment, a 1% gain each day for a year would bring the balance up to $37,409, while a 1% drop would reduce the balance to $26.
- A useful framework for understanding how to develop good habits is the Fogg Behavior Model. A detailed summary of this method, as applied to finances, can be found in Appendix D: Keys to Developing Better Financial Habits.
- The small habits we form are crucial because the little things are the foundation for the big things in our lives.
- The financial habits we want to cultivate are:
  - Prepare for the unexpected
  - Save for goals within two years
  - Pay yourself first
  - Spend mindfully
  - Pay down debt
  - Automate your finances
  - Take action

From Improving Our Habits
to Managing Risk

Just as Benjamin Franklin used the power of compound interest to turn $10,000 into $40 million, you can create good habits that generate exponential gains in your own financial life. One of the good habits we covered is preparing for the unexpected. This isn't just a good habit we want to cultivate. It's also related to the larger objective of managing risk in all forms, which is an essential component of financial serenity and spiraling up. That's why managing risk is the seventh and last principle we'll discuss and the subject of our next chapter.

Chapter 10

Principle Seven: Manage Risk

"Ignoring the risk and uncertainty in every decision might make us feel better in the short run, but the cost to the quality of our decision-making can be immense. If we can find ways to become more comfortable with uncertainty, we can see the world more accurately and be better for it."

> —**Annie Duke**, poker champion and behavioral decision science author, from *Thinking in Bets: Making Smarter Decisions When You Don't Have All the Facts*

"The essence of risk management lies in maximizing the areas where we have some control over the outcome while minimizing the areas where we have absolutely no control over the outcome."

—**Peter L. Bernstein**, acclaimed 20th-century financial historian, economist, and author of the 1996 book *Against the Gods: The Remarkable Story of Risk*

"Not taking risks one doesn't understand is often the best form of risk management."

—**Raghuram G. Rajan**, contemporary economist and former governor of the Reserve Bank of India known for his 2005 warning of the impending financial crisis

"A ship in harbor is safe, but that is not what ships are built for."

—**John A. Shedd**, 19th-century American author and professor

Dennis and Judy:
Two Great Retirement Options,
Paradoxically Loaded with Risk

Before they became our clients, Dennis and Judy, who were both 62 years of age, were agonizing over a decision. They couldn't decide whether to take his $1.6 million retirement account in a lump sum, or to choose $100,000 of guaranteed annual pension income for the rest of their lives.

Taking the lump sum would mean that their nest egg would be subject to market drops. On the other hand, taking the annual pension income instead would mean that their retirement would be at risk if Dennis's employer went bankrupt in the future. Taking the annual income would also mean they couldn't leave that lump sum amount to their kids. Either way, they would be taking a considerable risk.

Managing risk proactively is key, and the first step is to understand all the core areas of risk to manage.

There are three levels of risk in the risk management pyramid shown below. At the base, we have catastrophic risk, above that is savings risk, and investment risk sits at the top. It's critical to understand those risks and how to manage and protect yourself from each one.

We'll start at the base of the pyramid, which involves protecting yourself and your loved ones with various forms of insurance and an estate plan. While that may not sound sexy, it includes several vital components of risk management—some of which are too often ignored or overlooked. It's crucial first to ensure your pyramid has a strong foundation.

Then we'll move on to the next level of risk, which is building up and protecting your savings. Finally, we'll move to the top level of the pyramid and cover how to manage the risk in your investments.

Although Dennis and Judy came to us to answer a specific question about taking the pension in a lump sum versus a monthly income stream, we told them we couldn't answer that question without fully understanding their finances and risk tolerance.

To gain that understanding, we went through a discovery process to learn all about their financial life and concerns. Part of the process included evaluating all the risks they were facing, starting with the base of the risk pyramid.

Risk Management Pyramid

Investment Risk
Balance the risk of loss and inflation

Use proven risk management strategies to aim for the sweet spot of risk vs. return. If you must speculate, don't risk more than you can afford to lose.

Savings Risk
Build and protect your savings

Emergency fund: 3 to 6 months of expenses in FDIC-insured account. Save for large purchases planned within 2 years (vacation, car, home, etc.).

Catastrophic Risk
Protect yourself and loved ones from devastating events

Estate planning (wills, trusts, healthcare directives, etc.) and insurance (life, disability, property, and casualty).

The Catastrophic Level of the Risk Pyramid

The base of the risk pyramid is essentially protecting yourself and your family from unlikely but potentially catastrophic events. The best way to do that is through insurance and estate planning. Insurance compensates you in the event of an unforeseen occurrence or loss in exchange for paying a premium. You're exchanging the premium, which is a small, known amount of money you pay over time to cover a potentially significant, unknown loss. Estate planning is a process of anticipating and preparing for unforeseen or future events, like your incapacity or death.

Your Personal Financial Plan Encompasses the Following Four Areas of Insurance:

1. Life Insurance

Life insurance is indispensable if it's needed, but it's not always required. Whether or not you decide to buy life insurance is going to depend upon your circumstances. A couple who has a mortgage and children still living at home would be well advised to have a life insurance policy for both spouses.

In contrast, Dennis and Judy are empty nesters who have no debt and comfortably live off Social Security and their investment returns, so they don't need life insurance.

A family with a mortgage and young children would be wise to have at least enough life insurance on each spouse to pay off the mortgage if one of them were to die unexpectedly. That way, the surviving spouse could stay in the house and avoid uprooting the kids.

However, the need for insurance wouldn't stop there. It's a good idea to have enough insurance to cover the cost of the kids' college and to account for the lost wages of the deceased spouse. Using a withdrawal rate of 4%, $1 million of insurance would only replace about $40,000 of annual income. That means someone earning $80,000 per year should consider $2 million of life insurance to cover their earnings.

While that may sound daunting, simple term life insurance can be pretty inexpensive. For example, a $2 million policy on a 40-year-old man in excellent health may only cost around $130 per month. This would be for a 20-year term policy, meaning that he would pay premiums from age 40 to 60. The assumption is that by age 60, he has funded his retirement, he is nearly eligible for Social Security, and his children are no longer financially dependent on him.

Term insurance works a lot like car insurance. Just as he could pay auto insurance premiums for years and never get money back if he's not in an accident, he could pay life insurance premiums for those 20 years but not receive any payout if he doesn't die.

For that reason, some people look into buying permanent life insurance instead of term insurance. While permanent life insurance will eventually pay out as long as you pay the premiums, it can be drastically more expensive than term insurance. We generally don't recommend permanent insurance unless it is for complex estate planning needs for ultrahigh net worth clients subject to federal estate taxes.

2. Health Insurance

Without health insurance, you could be just one serious illness away from bankruptcy. In 2019, *American Journal of Public Health* published a study on medical bankruptcy. Of the 910 bankruptcy filers who returned their questionnaires, more than two out of three said their bankruptcy was due to medical bills, illness-related income loss, or both.

Covering yourself and your family with health insurance is vital for these reasons. Getting health insurance through your employer is generally the best and least expensive option. If employer-covered health insurance isn't available to you, getting group health insurance coverage through a professional association or organization may be possible. Another option is to buy private health insurance, and the Affordable Care Act (ACA) subsidizes the cost of those policies for lower-income families.

Many people don't know that Medicare eligibility doesn't begin until age 65, which can be an issue for those who want to retire before then. As Dennis and Judy were only 62, they found themselves in this situation. It wasn't an insurmountable problem, but we needed to help them carefully plan for their health insurance needs.

Health insurance cost them about $2,000 per month after they retired, so we created a budget item in their financial planning projections of $2,000 per month, from age 62 until Medicare began at age 65. ACA subsidies are based solely on income, not assets, so even wealthy individuals who retire early may find themselves eligible for a meaningful subsidy.

3. Disability Insurance

Many people think their most valuable asset is their home or car, but that's most likely not the case. For many, their human capital is their most valuable asset. A 45-year-old woman who earns $100,000 per year may earn $2 million if she works 20 more years until age 65. That capacity to work is most likely a lot more valuable than her home and car.

According to the Social Security Administration, the government paid disability benefits to almost 10 million Americans in 2021, and the average benefit was less than $1,200 per month.

Those statistics highlight two fundamental issues. First, disability causes many more people to be unable to work than is commonly thought. Second, Social Security benefits are not nearly enough to cover most people's living expenses.

One issue with private disability insurance is that it's much more expensive than term life insurance, but there's good reason for that. It costs more because it's more likely a worker in middle age will become disabled than die unexpectedly.

Like health insurance, getting disability insurance through employer benefits may be the least expensive way to go—however, there's one major drawback. If you lose your job, you'll also lose your disability insurance. If that's a concern or employer-sponsored disability insurance is not an option, you can buy a private long-term disability insurance policy.

For a 45-year-old who works in a low-risk environment, like in an office building, the rule of thumb is that private disability insurance would cost 1% to 3% of annual income. Let's assume 2% and that this individual makes $100,000 per year. She would pay around $2,000 per year for a disability insurance policy. This policy would cover 60% of her income until the age of 65 if she becomes disabled. Because she would pay the premiums with aftertax dollars, she would also receive the insurance benefits tax-free.

While $2,000 per year is a lot of money, it's possible to understand the trade-offs by reframing the decision as two options. Option 1 is a job that pays you $100,000 per year, but you would not receive any income if you were to become disabled.

Option 2 is a job that pays you $98,000 per year, but most of your income would continue, all the way until age 65, if you were ever to become disabled. Presented in this light, disability insurance may appear to be a shrewd investment to protect yourself from a low-probability but potentially disastrous event.

Buying disability insurance can be a great strategy to protect your human capital and future earnings. However, it's similar to life insurance in that it's not necessary for everyone. Dennis and Judy did not need disability insurance because they were on the verge of retiring.

4. Property and Casualty Insurance

This category covers areas like homeowners insurance, renters insurance, and auto insurance. Property insurance covers the things you own, like your home or car, while casualty insurance generally covers you for liability purposes. The liability portion is what protects you if you're sued and found to be legally responsible for an accident that injures someone or damages their property.

Homeowners, renters, and auto insurance policies typically include liability coverage, but that coverage has limits, which could be an issue. For example, an auto policy may have a liability limit of $500,000. If a member of your household were to be found legally responsible for a car accident that caused $800,000 of medical bills, your policy would not cover all those expenses.

That's where an umbrella insurance policy comes in. An umbrella policy provides extra insurance beyond the liability limits of your other insurance policies. If anyone ever said, "I'm going to sue you for everything you've got," that's where an umbrella policy would come in.

Imagine you had a $2 million net worth in the above example, and the injured person decides to sue you for all $2 million. If you had a $2 million umbrella insurance policy, that would cover your net worth. In other words, the court might award the injured person the $2 million, which your insurance company would pay to them. That way, you would keep the $2 million that made up your net worth (your home, retirement accounts, etc.).

Umbrella insurance is also relatively inexpensive. While Dennis and Judy had liability coverage of up to $500,000 in their homeowners and auto policies, they didn't have an umbrella insurance policy. We recommended they buy a $2 million umbrella policy, which would combine with their $500,000 liability coverage from their other insurance policies to cover their entire $2.5 million net worth.

The total cost of the umbrella policy was only about $300 per year. Even though they may never have to use the policy, that was a small amount of money for their additional peace of mind.

Estate Plans, which Form the Base of the Risk Pyramid along with Insurance, Generally Have Four Main Components:

1. Last Will and Testament

This is commonly known as a will, and it is one way to document who will receive your assets after you pass away. In some states, a will is subject to probate. Probate is the process whereby a court oversees the administration and distribution of your estate. A will is not probated in other states if it's part of an integrated estate plan that includes a trust. Also, a will allows you to nominate a representative, called an executor, who is one or more individuals responsible for carrying out your wishes and distributing your property.

If you have children under the age of 18, a will is paramount as it allows you to appoint one or more guardians to care for the children after your death. It's a good idea to update your will and the other components of your estate plan after any major life events, like marriage, divorce, death, or the birth of a child. It's essential to check the laws of your particular state and the legal requirements that apply to wills.

2. Trust Document

A trust is an agreement that outlines how, after you pass away, you want your estate administered and property distributed to your beneficiaries. A trust can be an agreement for one person or a married couple. A properly prepared trust in combination with a will (also called a pour-over will) can avoid a probate of your estate. Probates are time-consuming, lengthy, and expensive because a court is involved in the process. For many people, this is the main reason to create a trust.

A trust allows you to nominate a trustee or set of trustees who would oversee the administration of your estate and the distribution of your assets to your heirs. During your life and while you have capacity, you act as the trustee of your trust. When you die or become incapacitated, the trust lists persons you nominated to be successor trustees.

You could set up your trust to do things like pay for your children's college expenses if you were to pass away. Another option is to put rules in place so that after college, the trust would match your kids' earnings from their jobs each year, creating an incentive for them to work. You can use strategies like this to minimize the chances that your kids become the proverbial lazy trust fund baby.

If you have a will when you die but no trust, your estate may be probated, which, as mentioned above, is not only time-consuming but also expensive. Most probates require that a family hire a lawyer. In addition to the time and expense associated with probates, the information filed with the court in a probate becomes part of the public record, which results in your family losing its privacy. Creditors can easily find out about probates and use them as an opportunity to collect unpaid bills or bad debts.

The cost of setting up a trust can range from a few thousand dollars to tens of thousands of dollars for extraordinarily vast and complex estates. Trust and estate law is a unique practice area that not all attorneys understand, so you must use one who is experienced in it. The cost of a trust is well worth the expense because it is far less than the cost of probate. It is also possible to structure the trust to reduce or possibly eliminate estate taxes for larger estates.

3. Financial Power of Attorney

A financial power of attorney allows you to name one or more individuals to make financial decisions on your behalf should you become incapacitated due to an accident or illness. If you become incapacitated and don't have this document, there will be no one with the power to help take care of your financial affairs unless a court appoints a conservator.

A conservatorship, like probate, involves the court overseeing a person's affairs. Conservatorships are expensive and time-consuming. A financial power of attorney is an inexpensive way to mitigate the risk of a court getting involved in your finances, and it should be part of your integrated estate plan.

4. Advance Healthcare Directives

State laws vary regarding the type of document you need if you are incapacitated and can't make decisions about your healthcare. While the specific documents you'll need vary based on your state of residence, the goals of each are similar—to appoint one or more persons to make healthcare decisions for you in the event you become incapacitated. The two most common documents are a living will and a healthcare power of attorney. Both of these documents are types of advance healthcare directives.

A living will is a document used to give instructions to your healthcare provider in the event you are terminally ill, incapacitated, or unable to communicate. It outlines whether or not you would want to remain on life support or receive other life-sustaining medical interventions.

A healthcare power of attorney allows you to designate one or more individuals to make medical decisions for you if you can't make the decisions yourself.

The difference between a living will and a healthcare power of attorney is that the former outlines your specific wishes in writing, while the latter names a person who can act on your behalf to make those decisions. Advance healthcare directives should be part of every integrated estate plan.

Remember to check your state's applicable laws by consulting with an attorney specializing in trust and estate law. A poorly executed estate plan can have unintended consequences. As the old saying goes, "An ounce of prevention is worth a pound of cure."

Dennis and Judy's Estate Planning

Dennis and Judy had no estate plan when they first came to us, so we recommended they work with an estate planning attorney we have confidence in, based on her work with many of our other clients. The estate planning attorney created their will and trust to carry out their wishes and also developed custom financial and medical powers of attorney for them.

One of Dennis and Judy's concerns was that their son is not responsible with money. They were not worried about their daughter inheriting half of their $2.5 million estate. Their son, however, had struggled with drug addiction in the past, and they were concerned inheriting such a large amount of money could have unintended negative consequences in his life.

The estate planning attorney helped them craft a trust that first provided for their son's basic living expenses, so he would never be out on the street. The trust also allowed him to receive greater benefits from the trust if he continues to keep his addictive behavior under control.

They named Judy's brother as their successor trustee, which meant he would carry out Dennis and Judy's wishes if they died or became unable to manage the trust. They chose him because they knew he would be a great mentor and advocate for their son's well-being. These guardrails gave them peace of mind that their son would be cared for after they're gone.

The Savings Level of the Risk Pyramid

The next level up the risk pyramid involves savings. The most pressing need when it comes to your savings is to create an emergency fund. An emergency fund comprises cash you can quickly access in the event of an unanticipated expense, an illness, or the loss of your job.

We recommend having an emergency fund of three to six months in a safe, high-yield savings account. This account should be FDIC-insured and liquid, meaning the cash is readily available. If your income is unpredictable or unstable, it's a good idea to save closer to 12 months of expenses.

The next objective is to plan for short-term savings, which would include any purchases you may need to make in the next two years. For example, if you plan to take an extended vacation, buy a car, or make a down payment on a home in the next two years, you should set aside savings toward those goals each month.

These funds should also be in an FDIC-insured savings account. While it may be tempting to invest this money in stocks or bonds to earn a little money via a higher rate of return over the next two years, it's not a good idea.

Investing in stocks makes sense if you have a longer time horizon, but anything can happen in two years. You don't want to be in a situation where you save diligently for two years then suddenly lose 20% of your savings right before you need the cash.

Dennis and Judy had developed good savings habits over the years, and they had an emergency fund that would cover more than six months of living expenses. They also had a separate portion of their savings allocated to a vacation fund because one of their main goals in retirement was to travel more. The vacation fund allowed them to pay for travel with cash they had already set aside, so they could spend money on their vacations without feeling guilty.

The Investment Level of the Risk Pyramid

The top level of the risk management pyramid is investing, and we'll start by discussing long-term retirement investments.

Investing for Retirement

If possible, save at least 10% to 15% of your pretax income toward retirement each year and invest those funds with long-term growth in mind. These investments are considered long-term because they have the potential to grow for decades.

A woman in her 50s could have the funds invested in her retirement accounts for 40 years if she lives into her 90s. Younger investors have the potential to grow these savings for decades longer. That's why it's acceptable to take more risk in retirement accounts than you would in your emergency savings and short-term savings accounts.

While stocks can fluctuate up or down from one year to the next, the S&P 500 index, a widely followed basket of 500 large-company stocks in the United States, has always gone up over 30-year periods.

Ben Carlson, Director of Institutional Asset Management at Ritholtz Wealth Management, highlighted this in an interesting study. Even someone who had the misfortune of investing in the S&P 500 at the worst possible time, at the market peak just before the Great Depression, would have realized an almost 8% compound annual return over the following 30 years.

While the bulk of their retirement investments were in Dennis's $1.6 million retirement account, Judy had accumulated about $200,000 toward retirement in her IRA. She was concerned with how we would grow the assets while managing risk in that account. The $200,000 in Judy's IRA was also an important consideration when it came to deciding whether to take Dennis's pension as a lump sum or an income stream, as we'll see below.

Although I said above that it's acceptable to take more investment risk in retirement accounts, it can actually be necessary. The reason you need to take more investment risk is that without it, you're at the mercy of another stealthy, almost invisible, and inevitable risk: inflation.

Why Inflation Matters

Inflation is a general rise in the price of goods and services that leads to lower purchasing power of your savings. It's hard to believe, but a postage stamp in January 1991 cost $0.25. Thirty years later, in 2021, a stamp cost $0.55. That's an inflation rate of about 2.7% per year, which probably doesn't sound too bad.

But let's look at it another way. What if you had $0.55 thirty years ago, and today it is only worth $0.25? Again, that may not sound too bad. Now, let's put it in terms of your nest egg by multiplying both numbers by one million. What if 30 years ago you had a nest egg worth $550,000, and today it only had the purchasing power of $250,000? You would have lost over half of your purchasing power due to inflation. Alarmingly, that's likely to happen over the next 30 years if you were to hide your money under your mattress instead of investing in assets that grow.

Although nobody can predict future inflation rates, it is reasonable to assume that prices could double again over the next 30 years. We know that bank savings rates do not keep up with inflation, so it's smart to invest in other areas that do. Stocks are one of the best hedges against inflation over long periods of time because corporate earnings grow faster when inflation is higher.

This presents something of a conundrum. We are at risk of inflation over the long term if we don't invest in stocks, but we risk losing money in the short term due to market drops if we do. During the 2008 global financial crisis, the US stock market lost over 50% of its value, which was enough to scare countless investors out of the market.

However, US stocks recovered their losses by 2013 and have continued to grow since. In 2021, stocks are worth more than five times what they were worth during the global financial crisis, but someone who has stayed in cash since then has lost money due to the nearly invisible forces of inflation for over a decade.

That's why it's valuable to have a long-term perspective; it allows you to accept the risk of short-term loss to overcome the long-term effects of inflation.

Risk Management Strategies

In addition, by applying the risk management strategies outlined in the next section, it's possible to mitigate the risk of short-term losses. There are many strategies to manage the investment risk of stocks and bonds. Three of the most established strategies are asset allocation, diversification, and tactical asset allocation.

Asset Allocation

Asset allocation is the decision to weight your portfolio's investments to certain asset classes, like stocks, bonds, and money market. Bonds generally have lower short-term price fluctuations than stocks, which means they have lower market risk.

Although bonds are less likely than stocks to have large drops in value, they don't perform as well as stocks when inflation is high. Money market funds are one of the most stable asset classes. Similar to cash, money market has minimal market risk, but the real value of the investments can drop due to inflation.

You can initially determine your approximate asset allocation percentages using a risk profile questionnaire, generally a short quiz that helps determine how much risk you're willing to accept in your portfolio. Those with a higher risk tolerance will typically have a higher percentage allocated to stocks and a lower percentage to bonds and money market.

The opposite is also true. For example, someone with a moderate risk tolerance may allocate 60% to stocks, 35% to bonds, and 5% to money market. In comparison, someone with a conservative risk tolerance may allocate 40% to stocks, 50% to bonds, and 10% to money market.

Diversification

The second strategy to manage investment risk is diversification, which reduces your overall risk by spreading it across a large number of investments within each asset class. If your portfolio was 60% in stocks, but you only owned stocks in five companies, you would be placing yourself at considerable risk if one of those companies went out of business and the stock went to $0. A well-diversified portfolio may end up owning hundreds or even thousands of various company stocks and bonds through mutual funds or exchange-traded funds (ETFs).

Even though diversification can help, it still has its limits. Think back to 2008 and 2009, when the S&P 500 collectively lost over 50% of its value. The diversification of owning 500 stocks didn't protect investors from loss then, and owning hundreds or even thousands of stocks wasn't enough to protect investors during other severe market declines. That's where tactical asset allocation comes in.

Tactical Asset Allocation

Tactical asset allocation is a process of actively balancing and adjusting the percentages of the various asset classes within a portfolio. For simplicity, we'll use the three primary asset classes of stocks, bonds, and money market in this example.

The moderate investor above, who has a portfolio initially allocated 60% to stocks, 35% to bonds, and 5% to money market, would change those percentages over time. For example, when stocks are dropping during a market downturn, the mix may change to 20% in stocks, 35% in bonds, and 45% in money market. In other words, 40% moved out of stocks and into the money market fund.

The decisions to increase or decrease the percentage in the above asset classes result from investing models. One example of an investing model is price momentum. When prices in an asset class are trending upward, they generally tend to continue in an uptrend, so that would result in allocating more money to that asset class. Downward trending prices would result in moving money out of the asset class that's in a downtrend.

Another type of investing model uses relative strength. It's possible, for example, to measure the price trend of US stocks against the price trend of international stocks. When US stocks outperform international stocks, the model would recommend allocating more to US stocks and less to international stocks.

When evaluating tactical asset allocation strategies, it's important to recognize there are no free lunches in investing.

These strategies generally lose less money when the markets are going down and make less money when the markets are going up.

Therefore, a reasonable goal when using these tactical asset allocation strategies is to get to the same place financially in the end, but to get there with a smoother ride. Knowing there's a plan in place during the inevitable market downturn is sometimes all an investor needs to stay the course instead of panicking and selling at the worst possible time.

Risk-Adjusted Returns

The concept of risk-adjusted returns is simply a calculation of the investment's gain that considers the amount of risk necessary to achieve that gain. In other words, it measures how much you gained relative to the amount of risk you took to get it. Several measures can be used to calculate risk-adjusted returns for individual stocks, mutual funds, or even a diversified portfolio.

For this discussion, however, it's only necessary to understand that if two investments have the same gains over time, the one with the lower risk has a better risk-adjusted return. Let's consider the example of two investors who each earned 10% in a given year. If one of the investors earned that through a well-diversified portfolio and the other invested in a single volatile stock, the first investor would have received a much better risk-adjusted return.

The art and science of investing is about finding a suitable sweet spot in which you achieve an acceptable rate of return while minimizing the inherent risk. The acceptable rate of return is generally the return you would be able to realistically get while allowing you to reach your financial goals. Achieving that sweet spot is a dynamic process using the risk management strategies of asset allocation, diversification, and tactical asset allocation.

Speculative Investing

Unfortunately, the media has conditioned us to confuse investing with speculation, which involves a risk of substantial loss combined with a hope for substantial gains. Those who buy stock in an early-stage tech company without earnings—solely because a popular investment guru on television is pounding the table and honking horns screaming "Buy!"—are speculating.

While this is almost always risky, it might still be okay if you know this is speculating and not investing. The key is that if you're going to speculate, don't risk more money than you can afford to lose.

Generally, depending on your age, earning power, and temperament, this could comprise maybe 5% to 10% of your invested assets. For example, you might ardently believe in a handful of technology stocks or think cryptocurrencies are the future.

Before speculating with any amount of money, it's first necessary to build a solid foundation to your risk pyramid through insurance and estate planning, meet your emergency fund and savings needs, and use the recommended strategies to manage risk in your core investments.

The Elegant Hybrid Solution

This leads us back to Dennis and Judy's decision. They took our online risk tolerance questionnaire and both ended up in the moderate group. After discussing their risk tolerance and goals, we agreed a moderate investment allocation was an appropriate starting point.

However, they still had serious doubts about their decision to take the entire $1.6 million in a lump sum versus taking the income stream of $100,000 per year. Whatever decision they made with Dennis's employer was irrevocable. If they decided to take the $100,000 per year, they couldn't go back later and say they wanted to take the lump sum. Conversely, if they took the $1.6 million lump sum and lost it on bad investments, they couldn't go back and get the pension income stream.

The irreversible nature made it a huge decision. Dennis was leaning more toward taking the $1.6 million lump sum because he liked the idea of having a giant nest egg that they could tap in the event of an emergency. He also wanted to make sure they could leave a significant amount to their son and daughter.

Although he knew his company was in good financial shape today, he worried that taking the $100,000 annual pension could put their retirement at risk in the future.

He brought up the fact that Kodak was once a blue-chip stock, and it went bankrupt—almost unimaginably at the time—after the advent of the digital camera. What if his company experienced a similar, unforeseeable fate, and it couldn't continue paying the $100,000 per year decades from now?

Judy leaned more toward taking the $100,000 annually because she viewed it as a guaranteed income stream. She worried they could invest the $1.6 million in stocks and lose money, or they could live longer than expected, and their withdrawals over the years could reduce the account balance to zero. She argued that the $100,000 payments would continue for the rest of their lives, even if they both lived to be 110.

They didn't realize there was actually a third option. In fact, very few people know about this option because most financial advisors don't promote the idea.

Their decision didn't have to be all or nothing. We showed them it's possible to select the lump sum option and do a rollover of the entire $1.6 million into Dennis's IRA account. Then, we showed them how we could take a portion of his IRA and buy what's called a single premium immediate annuity (SPIA).

You may have heard that annuities have a terrible reputation in the financial services industry, and that reputation is well-deserved if you're talking about variable annuities. Variable annuities are incredibly complex products that charge high fees.

Not only are they difficult for even experienced financial advisors to understand, but they also lock investors into contracts for long periods. A typical annuity may charge surrender fees to penalize investors if they pull their money out within seven years of the initial investment, but penalties can last up to 15 years on some annuities.

A single premium immediate annuity is a very different type of financial product from a variable annuity. Because they don't pay high commissions, most advisors would never recommend an SPIA. However, they can be a great tool under the right circumstances.

An SPIA is a contract that allows you to pay an insurance company a lump sum up front, and then the insurance company makes periodic payments to you for the rest of your life or over a set period. This type of annuity dates back to the ancient Roman Empire—it's what annuities looked like before modern insurance companies began creating esoteric products designed to part investors from their money.

After reviewing our financial projections with Dennis and Judy and discussing several options, we agreed on a plan that addressed both of their concerns. First, we rolled over the entire $1.6 million into Dennis's IRA. They did not owe any taxes on this transaction because the funds were going from his pension into another tax-deferred account.

Next, we invested $1 million of Dennis's IRA in the stock and bond markets, using the risk management strategies of asset allocation, diversification, and tactical asset allocation.

With the remaining $600,000, we helped them purchase an SPIA that makes guaranteed payments of $36,000 per year. The SPIA began paying them immediately, and the payments will continue for the rest of their lives. Even if one spouse were to pass away, the income would continue for the rest of the surviving spouse's life.

We also invested the $200,000 from Judy's IRA in our diversified moderate portfolio. This resulted in them having $1.2 million in our managed investment accounts, which we invested to provide them with annual income. That also meant they would have a large amount of money available if they ever needed to take a lump sum in the future.

We were able to offer these options as a fee-only advisor because our recommendations were not clouded by the high commissions of questionable financial products. This hybrid solution allowed Dennis and Judy to balance guaranteed income with the liquidity of a large nest egg, along with the ability to leave a legacy for their children and grandchildren.

Summary of Key Points

- There are numerous risks when it comes to your finances, and the first step in addressing those risks is understanding what they are. Using the risk pyramid framework makes it possible to manage each risk you face, one by one.

- You can start by addressing the risks that could be the most catastrophic, even if they are unlikely to occur. For example, it's possible to manage the risk of premature death, unforeseen illness, and accidents by covering yourself with insurance and creating an estate plan to outline your wishes.

- You can then move up to the next level of the risk pyramid to ensure you are meeting your savings needs. First, by having an adequate emergency fund, then by making sure you're saving for things like a car purchase, vacation plans, or a home down payment that may occur in the next two years.

- Once those bases are covered, it's recommended that you begin saving at least 10% to 15% of your income, which you can then invest for retirement.

- When it comes to investing for your retirement, there are two primary types of risk you'll need to address: inflation and loss.

- The risk of inflation is invisible to most people, but it is very real. The way to manage that risk is to invest in assets that have the potential to deliver inflation-beating returns. That normally means moving away from CDs and bank deposits and moving toward stocks and certain types of bonds.

- However, stocks and bonds are subject to the other primary type of risk, which is the risk that your investments can at least temporarily go down in value. This risk keeps many investors up at night, but it can be addressed through asset allocation, diversification, and tactical asset allocation.

The Benefits to Dennis and Judy

By going through this process and systematically addressing all of the various risks to their financial future, Dennis and Judy were on a firm footing. This allowed them to make good decisions, leading to improved circumstances and better opportunities, which is our very definition of spiraling up.

Once they learned which types of insurance were necessary and which ones weren't, they were able to purchase a low-cost umbrella insurance policy that we recommended, along with medical insurance that would cover them until Medicare would begin at age 65. Even better, they stopped having that nagging feeling that they should look into the other types of insurance that they didn't need.

They also felt a tremendous sense of relief after completing their estate plan. Although the process led them to have some difficult conversations about their son and the potential return of his addictive behavior, they now know that they have every-thing necessary in place to help their children and grandchil-dren if something unexpected were to happen to either of them.

They already had an emergency fund and savings for their upcoming vacations when they met us, but going through our process together further reassured them that they were covered in those areas.

Outlining and discussing all of the risks associated with taking Dennis's pension in a lump sum versus the guaranteed income option gave them a clear understanding of the trade-offs with each option. This understanding allowed us to design an investment program that complemented their $36,000 stream of guaranteed annual income.

Over time, they also learned that managing risk is just one of the principles of financial serenity, and they eventually became familiar with the others. The following final chapter will illus-trate all of these principles with a remarkable true story.

Part III

THE PAYOFF: WHAT THIS ALL MEANS

Chapter 11

Lessons of a Lifetime

✓   Principle One: Focus On What You Can Control

✓   Principle Two: Accept That Wealth Is a State of Mind

✓   Principle Three: Cultivate a Growth Mindset

✓   Principle Four: Understand Your Personal Financial Statement

✓   Principle Five: Use Debt Wisely, and Pay It Off

✓   Principle Six: Develop Good Financial Habits

✓   Principle Seven: Manage Risk

A Heartbreaking Family Story

I have known my business partner and mentor, Bob Kargenian, since 1992. However, the story of our partnership began almost a century ago, all the way back in 1936. I hope you will find the story helpful as another real-life example illustrating the foundational principles of this book. It explains why for decades now, I have felt that financial planning is in my DNA.

My father was born in Centerville, Iowa, in September of 1936. Sadly, my biological grandfather, Claude Denzler, died of lobar pneumonia in June of that year, just three months before my dad was born. This was when the Great Depression was near its lowest point. My then 25-year-old grandmother had few skills and poor job prospects to care for my newborn dad and my then 19-month-old Uncle Norm.

Avis Blue Medland, circa 1930s

My grandmother Avis Blue Medland told an awe-inspiring story of loss, love, and joy in her unpublished memoir. She wrote about her entire life, starting in childhood, but one of the most poignant stories involved my grandfather's death. She wrote, "Three weeks before Claude died, a Prudential Insurance man called on me and sold me a small life insurance policy on Claude. I paid one quarter weekly, and for some unknown reason after I received the policy, he had not come back to collect for two weeks."

There she was, the literally penniless mother of a 19-month-old toddler, pregnant with her second child (my dad), and tragically widowed, all near the depths of the Great Depression in a year with a destroyed economy and near-record unemployment.

This was in an era when we didn't have the types of government support we have today. If she wasn't able to collect the insurance proceeds, she had nothing to fall back on. However, Prudential honored the policy, and she wrote, "I didn't dream I could collect from that policy, but they paid it in full—$250.00." That may look like an errant decimal place, but it's not; it is 250 dollars, which is an excellent reminder about the power of compounding and inflation.

This sum allowed the young widow to buy a home that sheltered her two babies and herself, and my dad never forgot that Prudential fulfilled its commitment.

Five decades later, in the 1980s, my dad hired his first financial advisor, who was, of course, at Prudential. When his first advisor left the firm for a competitor a few years later, my dad refused to leave Prudential out of loyalty for what they had done, despite his close relationship with his advisor. That advisor strongly recommended my dad work with a colleague named Bob Kargenian, which is what he did. The year was 1989.

When I graduated from college a few years later, I was earning a steady income as a US Navy submarine officer. That's when I began investing with Bob, based on my parents' recommendation. Having invested with Bob for seven years, I left the navy in the year 2000 to earn my MBA in finance at Wharton. Between my first and second year there, I did an internship with Bob, and he asked me to come to work with him full-time at Prudential after graduation.

Bob had also long been interested in leaving the firm and going independent. Although commissions accounted for less than 10% of his revenue, he didn't like the conflicts of interest associated with the commission-based model. We left Prudential together and founded TABR Capital Management in 2004, and we have served our clients as independent, fee-only advisors ever since.

It's always fascinated me that my grandfather's tragic death in 1936 precipitated this long series of events, eventually leading to my partnership with Bob.

From Desperate Struggle to Upward Spiral

In any event, my grandmother's memoir also highlights a number of important financial planning principles. There are elements of focusing on what she could control, recognizing that wealth was a state of mind, demonstrating a growth mindset, understanding her personal financial statement, minimizing debt, and exhibiting good financial habits. She also, of course, managed risk, which is why she received the $250 in insurance proceeds that was her lifeline during the Great Depression. I believe that following all these principles allowed her to spiral up into financial serenity and a better life.

She wrote in her book that after she received the $250 in insurance money, "I looked all over Centerville trying to find a small house for us and one day I drove up Orchard St. and saw the dirty little three-room house on the south side with three nice houses across the street on the north side. Someone had told me that house was for sale for delinquent taxes. I inquired at the Court House and found out that I could buy the house for $189.00, then wait 30 days and if the people didn't redeem it by then, I would be given the deed for it."

The house didn't have a telephone, sewage, or running water, but it was a roof over their heads, and my grandmother was even able to have electricity installed. Although it was far from a dream home, it would provide shelter.

They now had a place to live, but the insurance money had run out. My grandma didn't have money for adequate food or medicine for her children, and she suffered through some terrifying incidents. My uncle and dad were in the jaws of death as toddlers after they simultaneously contracted dysentery, a bacterial infection that spreads through contaminated food and water.

Even though my grandma couldn't afford to pay the doctor, he came to her home and the pair worked day and night to save her children's lives. She wrote, "Dr. Edwards was a struggling new doctor and needed the money, but he never turned me down in my life, and I vowed to him some day I'd rise above the position I presently was in." She would make good on that promise, although it would be a long road.

After she bought the home, she got a job doing office work in a law firm for $1.00 per day, which was considered good money for an unskilled worker during the Great Depression. She then worked for a short time in a factory wrapping butter that was cut by a machine, but she quickly realized she was not cut out for unskilled physical labor.

This was when my grandma's growth mindset began to emerge in her writing, although that specific term had not yet been coined. She knew that getting an education was crucial to lifting her family out of poverty, even though she didn't yet know how she would make that happen. In the early years, education meant learning how to help her young family survive, so her formal education would have to be delayed until her children were grown.

Her growth mindset was also evident in her knowledge that continuous small improvements would compound over time, and this belief began to manifest itself in her habits.

She made minor improvements to her home each year, like painting the exterior trim and buying a washing machine. The new washing machine required carrying buckets from a well and heating the water on an oil stove before emptying into the appliance, but it was a huge luxury compared with doing the laundry by hand.

The Family Grows

Then in the fall of 1938, she married my grandpa, Bill Medland, who would adopt my dad and uncle. They also had a son together, my Uncle Bill, in 1940. My grandpa was a coal miner and had sporadic income due to the seasonal nature of his work.

After the United States entered World War II in 1941, work became more plentiful, and my grandpa eventually got jobs in a factory, in a rock quarry, and at a foundry. He moved on to work in the boiler room for Iowa Southern Utilities, then worked on roadways for the Central Construction Company out of Indianola, Iowa, until he retired.

Even though they struggled greatly with money in the early years, my grandma always believed they could improve their living conditions through hard work and ingenuity. In her writing, she never blames others for their difficult circumstances. Instead, she was always focused on what she could control, recognizing the reality of the situation and determining what actions she could take to improve it. This focus allowed them to continue making those small advances over time.

A year after World War II ended, they added two more rooms on to their small three-room house. They did this by borrowing

$500 to buy an older home containing good lumber and tore it down to get the raw materials for the room additions. They saved money by doing most of the work themselves and paid off the debt as soon as they were able. That same year, my grandma also started a petition asking the city to put water in the neighborhood, and all of the neighbors got running water for the first time.

Living by Their Values

My grandma wrote of her belief in "progress in all activities in life" and was proud to have always been a "doer." She made a habit of taking action, no matter what she wanted to accomplish. In 1947, the first winter after having running water in their house, my grandparents worked with their neighbors to dig a basement under the home. The neighbors also banded together to dig a sewer below the basement and connect it to the city sewage system.

It took over 10 years, but by 1947 they had a home with electricity, running water, sewer, and a telephone.

My grandma watched every penny and developed good budgeting habits, always keeping expenses low. She didn't use the term "personal financial statement" in her writing. Still, she was keenly aware that maintaining expenses below their income allowed them to minimize debt and save for the future.

Fortunately, she didn't have to fight the siren song of social media in those days, but she had to contend with the budding consumer culture in the United States and the urge to keep up with the Joneses. In *The Price of Civilization*, a book by economist Jeffrey D. Sachs that discusses money, spending, and status, he says, "Living doesn't cost much, but showing off does." Thank goodness my grandma didn't care about showing off or social status. She focused on the essential rule to ensure more money is coming in than going out. At one point, they even took in a boarder to help cover their expenses.

Although she never wrote specifically about wealth being a state of mind, it is clear both from her writing and the stories she told me as a young boy that she truly believed that. She would recount to me and her other grandchildren story after story about life growing up on a farm and how she and her 13 (yes, 13!) siblings had everything they needed, even though they "were running around without a nickel in their pockets."

From the age of 17, she always worked to supplement her family's income, doing part-time work, odd jobs, and seasonal work, again demonstrating the habit of taking action. In her words, "Too often, the money would run out before I could meet all our needs, then I would worry. But I never stood still and worried. I got out and got a job and tried to keep things paid up."

Not only did she spend less than she earned and value financial independence over high social status, but she also saved for a rainy day. She and my grandpa further managed risk by having adequate insurance and an estate plan.

My Grandma's
Continued Education

After her two older sons left home, my grandma had the opportunity to get a formal education and improve her life even further. She enrolled in a junior college to become a teacher and graduated in 1957 at 47 years of age. That allowed her to begin teaching while she continued to take classes, eventually earning her bachelor of science degree in elementary education at age 53.

She went on to become the school principal, and one of her cherished possessions was her beautiful, solid oak principal's desk, which she was able to keep after she retired. Although we don't know exactly how old it is, our best guess is that it was built circa 1918. That coincides with the year the school opened, making the desk likely over 100 years old. My Uncle Norm preserved that desk for two decades after my grandma passed away and gave it to me two years ago.

Avis Blue Medland and Steven Wade Medland on July 4, 1972

As I sit at my grandma's prized desk writing today, I believe her financial values and principles served her well throughout her life. Following these principles eventually allowed my grandparents to make work optional, sell the Orchard Street home in 1970, and buy a new one. Their new home was a much larger and nicer five-acre Iowa farmhouse, located about 20 minutes away in the countryside. They never considered themselves to be "rich," but like Joseph Heller, they had something eminently more valuable: enough.

My parents and sister, our aunts, uncles, and cousins all spent halcyon summer days at the farmhouse when I was growing up. The kids especially loved exploring the nearby lakes, helping our grandpa mow the lawn on his rideable tractor, and chasing fireflies at night.

My grandparents lived there throughout their retirement and into their 80s. My grandma passed away in 1997, long before I became fascinated with the concepts of spiraling up and financial serenity. I never had the chance to ask if those ideas resonated with her, but had I asked her, I bet she would have said yes.

Epilogue

The Noble Path
of Financial Serenity

It is my greatest wish that you've found the stories and advice in this book helpful. Going forward, remember that you are fighting in an epic struggle against the evil forces of the media, consumer culture, social media, a deteriorating retirement system, and your own unchallenged limiting beliefs.

Let's start paying attention to the man behind the curtain, so you understand first that your anxiety around your finances is not your fault. These factors conspire to sabotage your financial success by subtly transferring your wealth over a lifetime to those who have power. However, that power is illusory as it is built on a general lack of knowledge. That means you can overcome it with the awareness you now have.

Let's name and demystify all of these forces, accept them as our adversaries, and thwart them by harnessing the positive forces found in the seven principles of financial serenity. Using these principles, combined with a mindset of gratitude, abundance, tranquility, and acceptance, you can and will overcome the system sabotaging your financial success.

This is your path to discovering financial serenity, making work optional, and living happily in retirement.

I hope you understand that your struggle is honorable and important, and once begun, it quickly becomes easier as you spiral up. You now have the knowledge and ability to prevail over these insidious forces as you embark upon the noble path of financial serenity. Only then can you understand that the joy of financial serenity truly exists and experience it for yourself.

Appendix A

Values Worksheet

Step 1: In the list of values below, circle the ones that resonate most with you:

Abundance	Generosity	Recognition
Accountability	Gratitude	Reliability
Achievement	Growth	Reputation
Authenticity	Happiness	Resilience
Autonomy	Harmony	Resourcefulness
Balance	Health	Respect
Boldness	Humor	Security
Collaboration	Independence	Self-Confidence
Commitment	Individuality	Self-Control
Community	Innovation	Self-Reliance
Compassion	Joy	Self-Respect
Consistency	Kindness	Serenity
Contentment	Knowledge	Service
Creativity	Learning	Simplicity
Curiosity	Love	Spirituality
Decisiveness	Loyalty	Stability
Dependability	Mindfulness	Strength
Determination	Motivation	Teamwork
Empathy	Optimism	Tranquility
Enthusiasm	Open-Mindedness	Trustworthiness
Equanimity	Organization	Understanding
Excellence	Passion	Uniqueness
Family	Peace	Versatility
Flexibility	Personal Growth	Warmth
Freedom	Playfulness	Wealth
Friendship	Presence	Wisdom
Fun	Quality	Zeal

Step 2: Using the values you circled, write down your top three values for each of the areas below:

Career	Community & Giving
1.	1.
2.	2.
3.	3.

Family & Relationships	Finance
1.	1.
2.	2.
3.	3.

Health	Recreation
1.	1.
2.	2.
3.	3.

Step 3: Based on the recurrence of values in your answers above, write your top three personal values:

My Top Three Personal Values
1.
2.
3.

Source: This Values Worksheet was created by adapting several sources, including the Carnegie Mellon University Values Exercise, Taproot.com, Power vs. Force: An Anatomy of Consciousness, The Hidden Determinants of Human Behavior by David R. Hawkins, MD, PhD, and The Minimalist Way by Erica Layne.

Appendix B

Recommended Reading

The following list of 50 books is in the approximate order that the book, or the author, appears in *Spiraling Up*. Although some of the books shown below do not appear in the text, they are all relevant to our topic.

1. *Principles: Life and Work* by Ray Dalio, 2017, Simon & Schuster

2. *Thinking: Fast and Slow* by Daniel Kahneman, 2011, Farrar, Straus, and Giroux

3. *The Behavior Gap: Simple Ways to Stop Doing Dumb Things with Money* by Carl Richards, 2012, Portfolio

4. *You Learn by Living: Eleven Keys for a More Fulfilling Life* by Eleanor Roosevelt, 2011, Harper Perennial Modern Classics

5. *Meditations* by Marcus Aurelius, 2018, The Stanford Encyclopedia of Philosophy, Editor, Edward N. Zalta, Metaphysics Research Lab, Stanford University

6. *The Enchiridion* by Epictetus, 1983, Hackett Publishing

7. *The Magic of Believing* by Claude M. Bristol, 1991, Pocket Books

8. *Thrive: The Third Metric to Redefining Success and Creating a Life of Well-Being, Wisdom, and Wonder* by Arianna Huffington, 2015, Harmony

9. *The 15 Invaluable Laws of Growth: Live Them and Reach Your Potential* by John C. Maxwell, 2012, Center Street

10. *As a Man Thinketh* by James Allen, 2006, CreateSpace Independent Publishing Platform

11. *Spiritual Economics: The Principles and Process of True Prosperity* by Eric Butterworth, 2001, Unity Village

12. *Flourish* by Martin E. P. Seligman, 2012, Atria Books

13. *Wherever You Go, There You Are* by Jon Kabat-Zinn, 2005, Hachette Books

14. *The Millionaire Next Door* by Thomas J. Stanley and William D. Danko, 2010, Taylor Trade Publishing

15. *Richer than a Millionaire: A Pathway to True Prosperity* by William D. Danko and Richard J. Van Ness, 2017, Million Dollar Press

16. *The Seven Stages of Money Maturity* by George Kinder, 2000, Dell

17. *Happy Money: The Japanese Art of Making Peace with Your Money* by Ken Honda, 2019, Gallery Books

18. *You Can Heal Your Life* by Louise Hay, 1984, Hay House

19. *Wooden: A Lifetime of Observations and Reflections On and Off the Court* by John Wooden, 1997, Contemporary Books

20. *Mindset* by Carol Dweck, 2006, Random House

21. *My Philosophy for Successful Living* by Jim Rohn, 2012, No Dream Too Big

22. *Man's Search for Meaning* by Viktor Frankl, 2006, Beacon Press

23. *Think and Grow Rich* by Napoleon Hill, 2005, TarcherPerigee

24. *Benjamin Franklin: An American Life* by Walter Isaacson, 2004, Simon & Schuster

25. *The Richest Man in Babylon* by George S. Clason, 2014, CreateSpace Independent Publishing

26. *Everything Is Figureoutable* by Marie Forleo, 2019, Portfolio

27. *Rich Dad, Poor Dad* by Robert Kiyosaki, 2017, Plata Publishing

28. *Born to Win* by Zig Ziglar, 2014, Word Wise

29. *The Elements of Investing: Easy Lessons for Every Investor* by Burton G. Malkiel and Charles D. Ellis, 2013, Wiley

30. *The Heart of the Buddha's Teaching* by Thich Nhat Hanh, 1999, Harmony

31. *Atomic Habits: Tiny Changes, Remarkable Results* by James Clear, 2018, Penguin

32. *The Life-Changing Magic of Tidying Up* by Marie Kondo, 2014, Ten Speed Press

33. *Tiny Habits: The Small Changes That Change Everything* by BJ Fogg, 2020, Mariner Books

34. *The Year of Less: How I Stopped Shopping, Gave Away My Belongings, and Discovered Life Is Worth More than Anything You Can Buy in a Store* by Cait Flanders, 2018, Hay House

35. *Moral Letters to Lucilius* by Seneca, 2011, Michael Hussey

36. *How to Win Friends and Influence People* by Dale Carnegie, 1998, Pocket Books

37. *Thinking in Bets: Making Smarter Decisions When You Don't Have All the Facts* by Annie Duke, 2018, Penguin

38. *Against the Gods: The Remarkable Story of Risk* by Peter L. Bernstein, 1996, John Wiley & Sons

39. *The Price of Civilization* by Jeffrey D. Sachs, 2012, Random House

40. *The Coffeehouse Investor: How to Build Wealth, Ignore Wall Street, and Get on with Your Life* by Bill Schultheis, 2013, Portfolio

41. *The Success Principles* by Jack Canfield, 2006, William Morrow

42. *The War of Art* by Steven Pressfield, 2002, Rugged Land

43. *Loving What Is* by Byron Katie, 2003, Three Rivers Press

44. *The Choice* by Edith Eva Eger, 2017, Scribner

45. *A Guide to the Good Life* by William B. Irvine, 2008, Oxford University Press

46. *The Minimalist Way: Minimalism Strategies to Declutter Your Life and Make Room for Joy* by Erica Layne, 2019, Althea Press

47. *Unshakeable: How to Thrive (Not Just Survive) in the Coming Financial Correction* by Tony Robbins, 2017, Simon & Schuster

48. *The Tools* by Phil Stutz and Barry Michels, 2013, Random House

49. *The Fourth Turning* by Neil Howe and William Strauss, 1997, Crown

50. *Ego Is the Enemy* by Ryan Holiday, 2016, Portfolio

Appendix C

Selecting a
Financial Planner

Michael Barry Carter:
Another Broker Pleads Guilty to Fraud

In the summer of 2020, Michael Barry Carter, a former Morgan Stanley broker in the Washington, DC suburbs, pleaded guilty to stealing over $6 million from his clients over 12 years. According to court documents, he forged clients' signatures and created false financial statements to cover up his theft.

The Securities and Exchange Commission (SEC) filed a complaint alleging that he defrauded victims, including an elderly client who was saving for her grandchildren's college expenses, to fund his own lavish lifestyle. He pleaded guilty and received a five-year federal prison sentence for his crimes.

Unfortunately, stories like this are all too common. Even though the financial advice industry is highly regulated, the rules alone won't protect investors from someone intent on defrauding them. It's up to investors to protect themselves, and though it takes a little bit of time and effort, it is possible.

The right financial planner is someone who is competent, ethical, and a good fit personally. You can find them by following some practical guidance, but before getting into specific recommendations, it may first be helpful to understand who can provide financial advice and who shouldn't.

Would You Ask Your Dentist to Perform Heart Surgery?

Before we unpack what a financial advisor is and isn't, this is a good time to talk about your CPA and attorney. While you ideally have a close working relationship with them, keep in mind neither received formal training in financial planning or investing for their accounting or law degrees.

While an intelligent professional whose work is adjacent to personal finance will learn a few things and much of the jargon over the years, they are not necessarily qualified to render financial planning or investment advice. This is true regardless of their professional demeanor and genuinely good intentions.

Think of your well-qualified fee-only financial planner as the quarterback of your personal finance team, with a competent CPA and estate planning attorney as valued linebackers and integral team members.

I am fond of my dentist of many years. He is ethical, highly competent, and an all-around wonderful man. But if I ever needed to have heart surgery, I would see a board-certified cardiac surgeon MD—not my dentist—because board certified means that he or she has completed years of exacting training, extensive supervised experience, and continuing education.

What Is—or Isn't—a Financial Advisor?

It's too bad that the term "financial advisor" is not regulated because anyone, even someone with absolutely no financial credentials, can use it. You'll also hear other creative terms such as financial consultant, wealth manager, investment consultant, etc. Because none of these terms actually mean anything, it's more useful to understand the standards that the various people who call themselves financial advisors follow or don't.

Financial advisors basically fall into two camps. The first group comprises brokers, who charge commissions, and it includes about 90% of the more than 300,000 financial advisors in the US. The second group encompasses registered investment advisors (RIAs), who charge fees and only make up about 10% of financial advisors in the US.

Commission-Only, Fee-Based, or Fee-Only?

Regulation Best Interest, or Reg BI, governs brokers. This is an improvement over their previous suitability standard, which only required they make recommendations that are "suitable." However, this is still a lower standard of care than the fiduciary standard, which RIAs must meet.

Reg BI requires brokers to disclose conflicts of interest, like commissions for selling a specific investment. It doesn't ban these conflicts, which means investors somehow have to figure out if brokers are actually working with their best interests in mind.

The fiduciary standard, by contrast, requires a duty of loyalty and care and ensures that an RIA cannot put their own interests ahead of their clients'. That's why it's so important to make sure you're working with an RIA before anything else.

Several decades ago, virtually all financial advisors charged commissions only, but many financial advisors didn't like the conflicts of interest associated with them. Imagine an advisor wanting to do the right thing for her clients, and the broker-dealer firm she works for (and that pays her salary) pressures her to sell the highest-commission investments to her clients. These investments may have been "suitable," but not the most suitable. By selling higher-commission products, she is putting her firm's interests above her clients', and therefore not acting as a fiduciary.

Due to this conflict, in 1982, a group of independent advisors got together in Atlanta, Georgia, to develop a better model to serve their clients. They discussed ways to provide investment advice that didn't require them to take commissions from the sale of financial products.

This small group of advisors then reached out to other advisors around the country to create what is now called the fee-only movement. In February 1983, this core group formed the National Association of Personal Financial Advisors (NAPFA) for RIAs who maintained a fiduciary standard and eschewed all commissions.

Fee-only advisors charge a fee to their clients for the advice and services they provide. This fee is usually based on a percentage of the assets they manage. However, some fee-only advisors charge hourly or based on completing a particular project, like creating an initial financial plan.

This fee is the same whether they recommend Investment A or Investment B, so the conflicts of interest inherent with commissions go away. In stark contrast, a broker may recommend Investment A over B if that were to pay them a higher commission. Individual investors liked the fee-only business model and began moving their accounts away from broker-dealer firms.

The fee-only movement was so successful that the large broker-dealer firms and Wall Street began to take notice. They then began to have their brokers register as RIAs so they could charge fees in addition to commissions. Because they were charging commissions and fees, they coined a shifty new term, "fee-based."

Many people believe fee-*based* and fee-*only* mean the same thing, but they do not. That's why you want to ensure your advisor is a fee-only fiduciary.

Only Fee-Only

If you start by selecting a fee-only advisor, you've already eliminated around 90% of the advisors out there and ensured you'll be working with a fiduciary. Still, that leaves tens of thousands of advisors in the country to choose from, so you'll need to narrow it down from there.

One of the best ways to find a fee-only advisor is to go to the NAPFA website (napfa.org), where you can search for advisors. Only about 4,000 of the country's fee-only advisors are NAPFA members.

NAPFA sets the industry's highest standards, by far. It is the only financial planning organization that requires a peer review of a financial planner's work before allowing them to become a member. A peer review ensures that the member demonstrates the ability to provide comprehensive financial planning. NAPFA also has the industry's most stringent continuing education requirements, requiring 60 hours of continuing education every two years.

Once you have a list of NAPFA advisors, there are a few other qualifications to consider. I mentioned that there are approximately 300,000 financial advisors in the United States. However, only about 88,000, or 29%, of those advisors are CERTIFIED FINANCIAL PLANNER™ (CFP®) professionals.

CFP practitioners are required to follow strict ethical standards, and only those advisors who have fulfilled the CFP Board of Standard's rigorous requirements can call themselves a CFP practitioner. In addition, a CFP professional must acquire several years of financial planning experience with clients and pass the comprehensive CFP Certification Exam.

There is an alphabet soup of other advisor designations out there, but many of them only require attending an afternoon seminar followed by a short written test. Some of these designations are more meaningful than others, but the gold standard in financial planning is the CFP designation.

If you're working with a CFP professional, you can look up him or her on the CFP Board of Standard's website (cfp.net) to verify their certification status and determine if they have a disciplinary history. Michael Barry Carter of Morgan Stanley was not a CERTIFIED FINANCIAL PLANNER™, so that wouldn't have helped much in his case—but that only strengthens the argument for working with a CFP professional.

Once you've reviewed the list of fee-only NAPFA advisors who have the CFP certification, you have a much shorter list and can look at those advisors' websites to determine if they offer the services you need.

After finding a few advisors who may be a good fit, you can then dig further to determine if they have any legal or ethical blemishes in their past. A great way to do that is to visit the SEC's Investment Adviser Public Disclosure (IAPD) website at adviserinfo.sec.gov. Just type in the name of the advisor and see if any disclosures appear.

Sometimes a disclosure will appear, but that shouldn't automatically eliminate the advisor from your consideration. Often these disclosures are for honest mistakes that the advisor made right, but at least you'll know about the mistakes and have the opportunity to ask the advisor about them.

The next step is to set up an introductory meeting with the advisor to meet with him or her in person or via video conference. With technology making video conferencing easy, it is more important to find the right advisor than the one who's in your neighborhood. This initial meeting will give you an opportunity to ask any questions you have about the services the firm will provide and the cost of those services.

You'll also learn who they use as a third-party custodian, like Fidelity or Schwab, which will hold your investment assets. Having your accounts with an independent custodian is for your protection because it makes it extremely difficult for an unscrupulous advisor to create false financial statements.

Bernie Madoff, the late perpetrator of the most extensive investment management Ponzi scheme in history, was able to get away with it for so long partly because he served as both advisor and custodian. This allowed him to make his account statements say whatever he wanted.

If you get pressure to sign up with a financial advisor, it is time to walk away. Take your time and make sure you feel like there's a good fit. You'll want to choose someone whom you enjoy talking with and is an attentive listener, because you're going to spend time together, some of which will be regarding highly personal and sometimes difficult decisions.

Summary of Key Points

I know it seems like a lot of letters, a veritable alphabet soup, but the bottom line is: if your lifelong financial health is as vital as your physical health, there is no need to settle.

There are hundreds of thousands of financial advisors in the US. Yet, those with all the proper credentials, certifications, and active professional memberships are few and will require some effort to find, qualify, and then determine whether they are a good fit for you personally.

Here is the checklist to use when selecting your financial advisor. Your financial advisor should be all of the following:

- 100% fee-only (not fee-based)
- A registered investment advisor (RIA)
- A CERTIFIED FINANCIAL PLANNERTM (CFP®) professional
- An active member of the National Association of Personal Financial Advisors (NAPFA)

- An active member of the Financial Planning Association®
  (FPA®)
- One who uses a third-party custodian like Fidelity or
  Schwab to hold your assets
- Willing to have a no-pressure introductory meeting with
  you to see if there's a good fit

The advisor should outline every one of these qualifications prominently in writing. An unwillingness to do so is a red flag.

Selecting a financial planner may initially seem daunting, but it's actually easy to do if you follow the above guidelines. In so doing, you'll be able to find a financial planner who is competent, ethical, and a good fit for you personally.

As a CERTIFIED FINANCIAL PLANNER™ professional, member of the Financial Planning Association, and long-time member of NAPFA, I am proud to report that I am routinely impressed with the majority of my true financial planner peers who have earned and maintain all of the industry's highest and most exclusive credentials. Don't settle for anything less, and I expect you will be impressed also.

Nobody wants to end up a victim of the next Bernie Madoff or Michael Barry Carter. As statistically unlikely as that may be, it is more likely you could get poor financial advice that effectively dooms your financial future to mediocrity or leaves you vulnerable to a major setback. Following this guidance will make it possible to avoid most of those pitfalls and find the right planner for you.

Appendix D

Keys to Developing Better Financial Habits

As mentioned in Principle Six: Develop Good Financial Habits, BJ Fogg has created a methodology of behavior change that can help us form better financial habits. His research shows that three variables drive our behaviors, and the diagram below shows how those variables relate to each other.

In the diagram, B = MAP means that a given Behavior happens when Motivation, Ability, and Prompt all occur above the action line in the same moment. Motivation is your desire to do a behavior, ability is your capacity to do the behavior, and prompt is your cue to do the behavior.

If your motivation is high and the behavior is easy to do at the moment you receive the prompt, you will do the behavior. If your motivation is low and the behavior is hard to do, you won't do it.

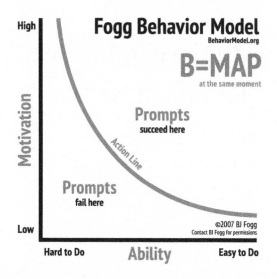

Source: BJ Fogg, www.behaviormodel.org. Used with permission.

If your motivation is high enough, you'll still do the behavior even if it's hard to do. Think of opening a can of chili without a can opener if you were starving. It may be hard to do, but you would find a way.

You'll also do the behavior even if your motivation is low, as long as it's easy enough to do. For example, you may not be highly motivated to support a particular charity that you had supported in the past, but what if they sent you a text that would allow you to make a small donation with two clicks on your phone? It's a lot more likely you would make the donation than if you had to dig out your checkbook and mail in a check.

In the same way, increasing your motivation and ability is vital when building good financial habits. That said, Fogg always recommends making something easier first, before trying to increase motivation. It's much more difficult to change behavior by increasing motivation alone. For these reasons, we'll discuss increasing ability (i.e., making something easier) first, and then we'll discuss increasing motivation.

Increasing Ability

Fogg discusses three broad paths to increasing ability. The first is training to increase skills, but that's the hard way. Another path is using a tool to make something easier, but that's not always possible. That's why the Fogg Behavior Model emphasizes and advocates the third option, which is scaling back the target behavior so it's easier to do.

To scale back the behavior appropriately, it helps to understand what's making the behavior hard to do in the first place. Fogg uses the Ability Chain model to show the five factors that make something hard to do. The five factors in the chain are: time, money, physical effort, mental effort, and routine. The weakest link in the chain determines what specifically makes something hard to do.

As an example, you might not be in the habit of reviewing finances because you don't have the time. If time is the weakest link in your ability chain, you may overcome that by deciding to only commit 10 minutes per week to review your finances. This is an example of scaling back the target behavior to make it easy to do.

As mentioned above, another path is to use tools that make the behavior easier to do. For this, I recommend using Mint. com, a free online tool that allows you to review all of your accounts at a glance. We'll discuss this further in the Creating a Prompt section below.

Another option is increasing skills. While that's the hardest of the three paths, it can be done—but that just means you'll need to have a growth mindset around your finances. If you believe you can cultivate your ability to manage your finances, you are more likely to make an effort to learn new things. This is especially true because the language of personal finance can sometimes be intimidating.

Regrettably, jargon is used intentionally in many professions to make things sound more complicated than they actually are. This illusion of complexity allows industry insiders to charge hefty fees to answer your questions or accomplish what you need.

The financial industry is also guilty of this, but you can develop your ability by reading personal finance books, including some of the books listed in Appendix B: Recommended Reading.

Reading personal finance blogs can also help make sense of financial strategies or concepts because they are often written by individual investors who've had to figure things out themselves. This frequently allows them to explain things in a way that is easy to understand.

The same goes for listening to podcasts, which is a terrific way to learn during your commute. It may also be helpful to simply look up financial terms online. Seeing the basic definition of a stock or a bond is a quick way to demystify such things.

Finally, if you'd like to understand the Fogg Behavior Model concepts better, you can sign up for a free five-day session with Fogg at www.tinyhabits.com/join.

Increasing Motivation

Many behavior change methods focus on increasing motivation as the key to change, but that's not as effective as you may have been led to believe. Because motivation fluctuates over time, you can't depend on motivation alone for behavior change.

When it comes to motivation, a more effective strategy is to find the right behavior for yourself. In other words, you can look for the helpful behaviors in which you already want to engage. The strategy of trying to motivate yourself to do something you don't want to do usually fails in the long run. Instead, try to discover a new lens through which you can look at your goals and make them more personally meaningful.

When it comes to your finances, there are several ways to do this, and they are related to having a clear vision of what you want. By clearly envisioning your ideal financial future, it becomes more likely that you will achieve your personally meaningful goals. You can do this through a variety of methods, including writing down your financial goals, using vision boards, visualization techniques, or affirmations.

Different people's brains are wired differently, so what works for one person may or may not work as well for another. A short description of each method is below.

Writing Down Goals

Vividly describing goals in writing is a top predictor of goal success. Something magical happens when you write down what you want instead of just thinking about it. Writing out your financial goals in great detail will give you more clarity about what you want and help motivate you toward achieving those goals. I discussed this method in greater detail in Principle Three: Cultivate a Growth Mindset.

Vision Boards

A vision board is an assortment of images representing your dreams or desires. If you want to live in a home by the water, your vision board could show pictures of your ideal home. It can also include favorite quotes or affirmations that will act as sources of inspiration and motivation. You can create vision boards digitally on computers and phone apps or use actual pictures on a poster board.

Visualization Techniques

Elite athletes and peak performers in all fields use visualization techniques. If you've ever seen an Olympic diver mentally rehearsing their next dive moments before getting on the platform, you've watched someone performing a visualization technique. Visualization can also help motivate you to achieve longer-term goals.

Jack Canfield, author of *The Success Principles*, says that visualization has four main benefits. First, it activates your creative subconscious, which helps generate creative ideas to accomplish your goals. Second, it programs your brain to find the resources needed to achieve your dreams. Third, it activates the law of attraction, which draws the people, resources, and circumstances into your life to help you attain your goals. Fourth, it builds your motivation to take action.

Visualization can take as little as five minutes a day. It entails finding a quiet place where you won't be disturbed, then closing your eyes and imagining what you want, just like it's on a movie screen.

Imagine whatever it is you're trying to achieve in as much vivid detail as possible. If you imagine that home by the water, envision the sights you would see, the sounds you would hear, and the feelings you would feel, all in bright focus.

Affirmations

After visualizing what you want, you can use affirmations to help bring it into reality. The method to do this is simple, but the science behind it is complex. Canfield explains that your brain has a network of neurons called a reticular activating system. It processes the millions of inputs you receive throughout your life, filtering out unnecessary information and allowing in the most important things. By giving your mind a crystal-clear image of what you want, you're priming your brain to recognize opportunities and circumstances that will bring your vision into reality.

If you've ever set a goal to, for example, have an extended vacation in Ireland, and you randomly meet someone at a party who founded an Ireland travel blog, that's your reticular activating system at work. Your mind filtered out all the noise at the party, and you "just happened" to meet the one person there who loves Ireland and can't wait to share their travel tips, ways to save money, and favorite spots in Ireland with you.

The simple affirmation Canfield teaches is, "I am so happy and grateful that I am now . . ." After visualizing that home on the water, you could say, "I am so happy and grateful that I am now enjoying living in my dream home on the water." This is short, specific, positive, and in the present tense, as if it's already happened. Creating affirmations in this way will put your reticular activating system to work in your subconscious, even when you're not actively thinking about your goals.

Creating a Prompt

Remember that the B = MAP formula says a behavior will happen when motivation and ability are high enough in the instant that the prompt occurs.

In other words, prompts succeed when you're both motivated and able to do the behavior; prompts fail when either one of those things is not true. The most effective prompts are tied to a reliable, already existing behavior or something that easily fits into your routine.

Applied to personal fitness, someone who wants to get in better health may set a goal to walk two miles in the morning. If their motivation to be in better health is high and they have the ability to walk two miles, they will perform that behavior as long as they have the correct prompt.

One way to create that prompt is by placing their walking shoes and clothes right next to their bed, so they'll see them as soon as they wake up in the morning. This is an example of tying a prompt (seeing walking shoes) to an already existing behavior (getting out of bed). When they get up and the first thing they see is that prompt next to their bed, they're going to go on that walk because their motivation and ability are both there.

Similarly, after you've increased your motivation and ability to improve your finances using the methods discussed above, you can also choose to create a prompt that works for you. I recommend you set aside a specific time to review your finances one day each week.

The key is to make the prompt effective by tying it to an existing behavior, putting that time on your calendar, or setting a reminder on your phone. I also recommend doing the review using something like Mint.com, as mentioned above. If you do this consistently, you don't need to spend a lot of time on it each week.

Remember, it's helpful to set the ability bar low; that way, you can perform the behavior even when your motivation is flagging. You can just commit to reviewing your finances for 10 minutes to ensure everything is on track.

The focus should be on evaluating assets, liabilities, income, and expenses, which I discussed in Principle Four: Understand Your Personal Financial Statement. For example, is your income higher than your expenses? If so, is that positive cash flow being effectively channeled toward paying down debt or buying income-producing assets?

If you're only committing to 10 minutes, it's hard to use lack of time as an excuse. And the beauty of this strategy is that often after the 10 minutes are up, you may be enjoying the process and decide to spend a little more time on the review.

Let's say you decide on 8:00 a.m. each Friday morning, the one day each week when you have your morning cup of coffee at your favorite coffee shop. This is another example of tying a prompt to an existing behavior. If you'd like, you can also either set up a recurring calendar event or a reminder on your phone.

At that time, you can log into your Mint.com account and review the dashboard. The program shows graphically where your spending is compared with your income. It also allows you to create a customized budget, develop savings goals, and manage your debt. This provides a snapshot of where your finances are at any given time, and it's a great way to track the results of your good financial habits.

Following is a screenshot from Mint.com showing a hypothetical family's balance sheet. By clicking on the arrow next to each category (Cash, Credit Cards, Loans, etc.), they will see the details of each. For example, if they click on Loans, they'll see the approximately $400,000 mortgage balance for their residence along with their $200,000 mortgage balance for their condo rental property.

The same is true if they click on their Property tab, which will break down their $1.1 million residence along with their $500,000 condo rental property. This is an easy way to review assets and liabilities at a glance, and it doesn't take more than a few minutes if you do it consistently.

The advantage of using something like Mint.com is that you can log in with one username and password instead of having to log in separately to view your credit card transactions, checking account activity, and mortgage balance, in addition to all of your other various accounts.

You can also set up customized budgets, allowing you to track income and spending in various categories. In other words, you have access to view your four main financial levers: income, expenses, assets, and liabilities, conveniently in just a few minutes.

ACCOUNTS	⚙
> 🔲 Cash	$9,427.86
> ▭ Credit Cards	-$906.88
> 🎓 Loans	-$606,272.23
> ▯▯▯ Investments	$717,507.55
> 🏠 Property	$1,602,385.00
ASSETS	$2,329,320.41
DEBTS	-$607,179.11
NET WORTH	$1,722,141.30

Sample screenshot from Mint.com

Getting into the habit of viewing these details regularly enables you to facilitate the upward spiral discussed in detail in Principle Four: Understand Your Personal Financial Statement.

Celebrating Small Wins

After you finish reviewing your finances, it's a great idea to celebrate the steps you've taken to get closer to your financial goals.

In *Tiny Habits*, BJ Fogg recommends celebrating immediately and with joyful intensity. He writes:

> Celebration will one day be ranked alongside mindfulness and gratitude as daily practices that contribute most to our overall happiness and well-being. If you learn just one thing from my entire book, I hope it's this: celebrate your tiny successes. This one small shift in your life can have a massive impact even when you feel there is no way up or out of your situation. Celebration can be your lifeline.

Celebrating in the ways he recommends may sound silly, but it works. You could look in the mirror and say something like, "You got this!", "Yes!", or "You are awesome!" Or, you could simply smile widely, do a fist pump, and imagine the roar of the crowd.

As Fogg said, "When I teach people about human behavior, I boil it down to three words: emotions create habits. It's not repetition or frequency, as others have suggested. That's why celebration is so important; it creates the positive feelings that wire in new habits."

Getting and celebrating small wins, like a quick review of your finances, is both fulfilling and self-reinforcing; it feels so good that you'll want to do it again the following week. That creates a positive feedback loop by increasing your motivation, and the time invested reviewing your finances simultaneously increases your ability.

Summary of Key Points

- Behavior happens when Motivation, Ability, and Prompt all converge at a single point in time. This can be expressed by B = MAP. Higher motivation and making a behavior easier to do lead to performing the desired behavior and better outcomes.
- The Fogg Behavior Model emphasizes making something easier first before trying to increase motivation because it's much more difficult to change behavior by increasing motivation alone.
- You can increase ability by scaling back the target behavior to make it easy to do. This is the preferred path, and an example is only committing 10 minutes per week to review your finances.

- You can also increase ability by using tools like Mint.com, which makes the behavior easier to do.
- Finally, you can increase ability by increasing skills. While this is the most challenging of the three paths to make something easier, it can be done. This is related to having a growth mindset around your finances, reading personal finance books and blogs, or listening to finance podcasts.
- Trying to increase motivation to do something you don't want to do is not effective. Instead, try to discover a new lens through which you can look at your goals to make them more personally meaningful. You can do this by envisioning your ideal financial future, which can be done by writing out your goals, using vision boards, visualization, or affirmations.
- Once your motivation is at higher levels and you make the behavior easier to do, you can create an effective prompt by scheduling a short amount of time to review your finances each week. This is most effective when you tie the prompt to an already existing behavior, like your weekly visit to your favorite coffee shop.
- Celebrating small wins will reinforce your good financial habits, and sometimes all that takes is verbally or literally patting yourself on the back.

Acknowledgments

Writing this book has been a roller coaster, and I couldn't have done it without the most important people in my life. This includes my family, friends, colleagues, and clients, but it all started with my parents.

Thanks, Dad, for always being a great example to me when it came to finances—and in every other way. I still remember you explaining to me at a young age how compound interest works. And I'll always be grateful that you instilled the belief in me that it's possible to be financially successful with the right plan, self-discipline, and enough time.

Mom, thank you for teaching me that contentment is better than riches, both through your words and actions. You and Dad embody all of the principles in this book, and I appreciate that you both took the time to read the manuscript and give me so much valuable feedback.

To my business partner, Bob Kargenian, thank you for your never-ending support, counsel, and patience throughout the long process of writing this book. And to Mary Hernandez and Sylvia Bazan, our wonderful office manager and administrative assistant, thank you both for assisting me when I was writing the book and needed extra help serving our clients.

To my editor, John Shaw, I can't thank you enough for your guidance on this journey. When I first handed you the dumpster fire that was my first draft, you said, "It needs a lot of work." That was an understatement. When I later got so discouraged that I almost couldn't continue, you became my de facto coach and helped me see the way forward. Thank you for your words of advice and encouragement. This book wouldn't be what it is without you.

Several people whom I trust and admire were a huge help by agreeing to read the near-final manuscript and give me feedback. Thank you to one of my best friends, Glenn Hamburger, not just for your advice on the manuscript but also for always encouraging me to keep going during the times when the project would inevitably get derailed.

Thank you, Sarah Sword, for using your incredibly sharp intellect to find inconsistencies in the manuscript and help make it flow. Jessica Losch, I sincerely appreciate you taking the time to read the manuscript and give me your insightful comments. You looked at it from a fresh perspective, and the book is better for it.

Thank you also to Izzie Lannan, whose love and support were

critical during the long adventure of writing this book. Not only did you point out areas for improvement in the manuscript, but you also let me talk endlessly about the stories and ideas in each chapter, allowing me to work through concepts by thinking out loud. Many of the breakthroughs I had resulted from these long discussions. You never once asked me to change the subject or talk about something else, even though I could not have blamed you if you had.

A special thanks to Jeffrey Resnick, a skilled estate planning attorney who has helped a number of my firm's clients. Your advice regarding estate planning language in the book was invaluable.

Thank you to Tanna Drapkin, Lab Manager of the Stanford Behavior Design Lab, for your guidance and feedback regarding the BJ Fogg Behavior Design Model. Your comments and advice allowed me to present BJ's work in the most accurate and helpful way.

I'd also like to thank my longtime graphic designer, Paula Doubleday, who designed the book's graphics to make these concepts easier to understand.

Finally, I feel compelled to thank someone I've never met, but without whom I may have never finished this book. Steven Pressfield is a fellow veteran and a writer's writer. He is well-known for his works of fiction, and he is also the author of the nonfiction classic *The War of Art: Break Through the Blocks and Win Your Inner Creative Battles* (2002). More than any other book, *The War of Art* helped me understand and overcome a force he calls Resistance, which disrupted my efforts to write this book for years.

Unfortunately, after overcoming that Resistance and finishing my first draft of the manuscript, I realized it wasn't very good (see dumpster fire, above). That's where another one of his books, *Nobody Wants to Read Your Sh*t: Why That Is and What You Can Do About It* (2016), came in. His book helped me hone the structure and concept of my book, improving it immensely. Steven Pressfield, you may never read this, but if you do: *Thank you.*

About the Author

While most high school students were dreaming about the day they get their driver's license, Steve was already investing in the stock market with his father's guidance. Growing up in Orange County, California, his parents stressed the importance of savings; however, money was tight when it came time to apply for college. Undaunted, he applied for and received a congressional nomination and full scholarship to the US Merchant Marine Academy at Kings Point, New York. Equipped with his engineering degree after four years at the academy, he set his course for a new destination: navy submarine officer.

Though Steve was only earning about $24,000 per year initially after graduation, he immediately started saving $150 per month and investing it in the stock market. Applying the discipline he developed in the navy, he took at least half of the monthly increase from each raise and promotion and added it to his investments. This tactic eventually allowed him to leave the navy to fund and pursue his interest in finance by earning an MBA from the Wharton School.

While Steve was earning his MBA, the internet bubble collapse was creating market havoc. He contacted his financial advisor, Bob Kargenian at Prudential, and asked to spend the summer of 2001 interning and analyzing Bob's approach to business with the tools Steve had developed in business school.

During that summer, he experienced the difference between generic financial advice and well-researched financial planning and how the latter could lead to a far more secure and rewarding life. It was then that he realized financial planning was no longer just a personal interest, but his calling.

The two had a productive summer together, and after Steve graduated, Bob brought him on board. After a year of working together, the pair co-founded TABR in 2004.

Steve's strategic and tactical approach to financial planning has made him a reliable source for insights into market trends. He has been quoted in *The Wall Street Journal*, *Reuters*, *BusinessWeek*, *Newsweek*, *US News & World Report*, and *Kiplinger's Retirement Report*, among others.

Steve is also a regular guest financial planning expert for the *Your Money* radio program on SiriusXM Radio.

He is a CERTIFIED FINANCIAL PLANNER™ professional, member of the National Association of Personal Financial Advisors (NAPFA), and the Financial Planning Association® (FPA®).

Steve writes about financial planning and the pursuit of financial serenity at stevemedland.com.

Giving back is an essential part of Steve's life. He has helped build seven homes with Habitat for Humanity and currently volunteers with Homes for Our Troops, an organization that builds specially adapted homes for severely injured veterans. He is also a volunteer interviewer for the University of Pennsylvania/Wharton School Alumni Interview Program.

Steve enjoys traveling, sailing, and hiking with his family, and practicing Krav Maga.

Did reading *Spiraling Up* help you in some way?

If it did, I'd love to hear your thoughts.
Honest reviews help readers find the right book
that can help them as well.
Thank you.

Made in the USA
Las Vegas, NV
29 March 2022

46512504R00173